Lecture Notes
in Business Information Processing 467

LNBIP reports state-of-the-art results in areas related to business information systems and industrial application software development – timely, at a high level, and in both printed and electronic form.

The type of material published includes

- Proceedings (published in time for the respective event)
- Postproceedings (consisting of thoroughly revised and/or extended final papers)
- Other edited monographs (such as, for example, project reports or invited volumes)
- Tutorials (coherently integrated collections of lectures given at advanced courses, seminars, schools, etc.)
- Award-winning or exceptional theses

LNBIP is abstracted/indexed in DBLP, EI and Scopus. LNBIP volumes are also submitted for the inclusion in ISI Proceedings.

Jos van Hillegersberg · Jörg Osterrieder ·
Fethi Rabhi · Abhishta Abhishta ·
Vijay Marisetty · Xiaohong Huang
Editors

Enterprise Applications, Markets and Services in the Finance Industry

11th International Workshop, FinanceCom 2022
Twente, The Netherlands, August 23–24, 2022
Revised Selected Papers

Springer

Editors
Jos van Hillegersberg ⓘ
University of Twente and JADS
Enschede, The Netherlands

Jörg Osterrieder ⓘ
University of Twente
Enschede, The Netherlands

Fethi Rabhi ⓘ
University of New South Wales
Sydney, NSW, Australia

Abhishta Abhishta ⓘ
University of Twente
Enschede, The Netherlands

Vijay Marisetty ⓘ
University of Twente
Enschede, The Netherlands

Xiaohong Huang ⓘ
University of Twente
Enschede, The Netherlands

ISSN 1865-1348   ISSN 1865-1356 (electronic)
Lecture Notes in Business Information Processing
ISBN 978-3-031-31670-8   ISBN 978-3-031-31671-5 (eBook)
https://doi.org/10.1007/978-3-031-31671-5

This Springer imprint is published by the registered company Springer Nature Switzerland AG
The registered company address is: Gewerbestrasse 11, 6330 Cham, Switzerland

Preface

Now in its eleventh consecutive year, FinanceCom 2022 was held for the first time in the Netherlands, hosted by the Section Industrial Engineering and Business Information Systems of the Department of High-Tech Business and Entrepreneurship at the University of Twente, August 23-24, 2022. This came after very successful FinanceCom workshops in Sydney (twice), Regensburg, Manchester (UK), Montreal, Paris, Frankfurt (twice), Barcelona, and online.

This event has become truly international, with participants and speakers from thirteen countries, including the USA, Kenya, and Australia. The University of Twente hosted 50 participants from the Netherlands and the rest of Europe, in addition to 30 distinguished academic and business speakers. The conference brought together policymakers, national and European academics, and technology and financial services industry participants, and served as a forum for interdisciplinary discussion and the exchange of ideas regarding the adoption of innovative technologies in the financial services industry.

This year, the conference was also supported by the European Union under the COST (Cooperation in Science and Technology) scheme, the longest-running European intergovernmental framework for cooperation in science and technology. The COST Action CA19130 Fintech and Artificial Intelligence is a research network connecting 270+ researchers from 49 countries globally.

Themes and Key Topics of FinanceCom 2022

Information technology advancements not only alter the manner in which we communicate and process data, but also pave the way for new business models, markets, networks, services, and players in the financial services industry. Some of these developments include electronic trading, data analytics, and fintech services. Since its inception, the FinanceCom conference series has provided significant academic research in this area at the intersection of information systems and finance, well before the emergence of the finfech concept. The research presented at FinanceCom conferences aims to assist academics and practitioners in comprehending, driving, and capitalizing on the opportunities presented by these information technology-driven financial sector developments.

The conference featured four main themes: Networks and Business Models, Financial Markets, IT and Implementations, and New Emerging Digital and Virtual Financial Markets. The first theme, Networks and Business Models, focused on the ways that financial institutions are connected to each other and how these connections affect their business operations. The second theme, Financial Markets, explored the latest trends and developments in financial markets, including the rise of fintech and the impact of digital technologies on financial services. The third theme, IT and Implementations, examined the role of information technology in the finance industry and the challenges and opportunities of implementing new technologies. The fourth theme, New Emerging

Digital and Virtual Financial Markets, looked at the ways that digital and virtual financial markets are changing the way that financial services are delivered.

The topics covered some of the latest advances and techniques from academia and the financial industry: blockchain, financial sentiment analysis, stress tests, stock price predictions, fintech loans, Internet measurements for finance, an e-invoicing ecosystem, mobile payments, financial intermediary misconduct, machine learning, interest rate regulations, AI ethics, systemic risks, sustainability goals, Big Tech firms, generative adversarial networks, explainable artificial intelligence, the Digital Art Index, AI-enabled decision systems, an effective analytics organisation, digital payments, corporate regulatory exposure, and a data analytics framework.

FinanceCom 2022 resulted in fruitful discussions about the presented papers and an exchange of ideas with participants joining our conference from Australia, Europe, and the United States, physically at the University of Twente.

Conference Proceedings

We received 25 submissions for this first post-Covid FinanceCom workshop, from which we chose eight high-quality papers to be published in this volume after revision. The selection was based on a rigorous review process carried out with the assistance of a program committee of internationally renowned researchers in the field, who also significantly contributed to the improvement of the selected papers through comments and suggestions.

The first paper, "A data analytics architecture for the exploratory analysis of high-frequency market data," authors Siu Lung Ng and Fethi Rabhi, proposes a design for an architecture that aims to reduce the technical challenges associated with analyzing high-frequency market data. The availability of high-frequency data has become increasingly important in fields such as econometrics, finance, and accounting, but the analysis of such data requires a combination of domain knowledge and IT expertise. The proposed architecture integrates data acquisition, analytics services, and visualization to make it easier for researchers and domain experts to perform ad hoc analysis of high-frequency data.

The second paper, "Give Them a Second Chance? Prediction of Recurrent Financial Intermediary Misconduct" by Jens Lausen and Benjamin Clapham presents a valuable contribution to the literature on financial misconduct and automated fraud detection. The authors develop predictive models to identify brokers that commit misconduct multiple times. The paper is based on a comprehensive dataset and is valuable for investors and regulators alike, as it can assist in identifying and preventing recurrent financial intermediary misconduct.

The third paper, "A Framework to Measure Corporate Regulatory Exposure" by Jascha-Alexander Koch and Peter Gomber presents a useful approach for companies to determine the relevance of regulations in an automated manner. The authors argue that the growing and changing corpus of regulations presents a challenge for companies, as it is difficult for them to identify which regulations apply to their business activities. To address this problem, the authors propose a decision support framework that uses natural language processing techniques to identify relevant regulations. This framework is applied to the US Code of Federal Regulations, and the results are discussed in the paper.

The fourth paper, "Realising Value from AI-Enabled Decision Systems with Fair Outcomes: An Exploratory Case Study" by Franziska Koefer, Ivo Lemken, and Jan Pauls is an important contribution to the growing body of literature on the ethics and fairness of AI. The authors argue that despite the increasing consensus on principles of fairness in AI, there is a gap between the potential and actual realized value of AI due to a lack of practical guidance on how to apply these principles in real-world settings. To address this gap, the authors propose a framework for organizations to consider throughout the AI product life cycle, from design and development to deployment and maintenance, in order to ensure fair outcomes. The framework is based on a case study of a social impact microfinance organization that uses AI-enabled credit scoring to support the screening process for financially marginalized entrepreneurs.

The fifth paper, "The effect of changes in interest rate regulation on the financial performance of banks in Kenya" by Jane Ngaruiya, Pat Obi and David Mathuva aims to assess the impact of changes in interest rate regulation on the financial performance of banks in Kenya. Interest rate is an important macroeconomic variable that is directly related to economic growth. The imposition of interest rate controls has been a common practice in many countries, including Kenya, in the aftermath of the Global Financial Crisis (GFC) of 2008-2009. However, the effects of such regulations on the economy are not well understood, and previous studies on the subject have been relatively sparse. The authors conclude that their study provides evidence in favour of the imposition of interest rate controls to regulate lending rates charged by commercial banks.

The sixth paper, "Towards an API marketplace for an e-invoicing ecosystem" by Chinmay Manchanda, Walayat Hussain, Latif Rabhi, and Fethi Rabhi presents a solution to the challenges faced by e-invoicing solution providers. E-invoicing has become increasingly popular as a means of streamlining the billing process and reducing the risk of errors and fraud. However, the adoption of e-invoicing is also creating new challenges, such as compliance with regulations, cross-border issues, and the need to support multiple standards and formats. The authors' proposed solution shows potential for addressing the complexities of e-invoicing regulations and standards, and their preliminary results indicate the feasibility of the approach.

The seventh paper, "Role of culture in customer acceptance of neobanks" by Koen Meijer, Abhishta Abhishta and Reinoud Joosten analyzes the role of Hofstede's cultural dimensions in the acceptance of Neobanks. Recent years have seen a surge in the number of fintechs including fully online banks, referred to as Neobanks. However, acceptance of these banks varies among different countries and continents. This paper includes culture (as Hofstede's cultural dimensions) as part of the technology acceptance model (TAM) to investigate its role in the acceptance of neobanks. Based on a survey of Neobank users, this paper finds that the original constructs of TAM and 'Trust' have a positive impact on the acceptance of Neobanks.

The eight paper, "From Perceived Mobility to the Intention to Use Mobile Payments: The Role of Positive and Negative Determinants" by Petar Dzelalija and Ana Ivanisevic Hernaus presents a valuable contribution to the understanding of the factors that drive consumer adoption of mobile payments. The paper departs from the traditional TAM and TRAM frameworks and incorporates additional determinants such as perceived mobility and trust. The authors use a sample of 218 financially educated individuals to examine the predictive role of mobile payment antecedents and find that mobile payment knowledge mediates the relationship between perceived mobility and intention to use mobile payments. The paper also highlights the moderating roles of perceived compatibility and perceived risk.

The authors' ability to validate their comprehensive research model and extend the demographic and regional scope of the related research adds to the value of the paper. Overall, this paper provides insights into the underlying mechanisms and boundary conditions driving consumers' decision to use mobile payments for everyday transactions. Policymakers and businesses seeking to promote the adoption of mobile payment technologies can benefit from the implications of the study's findings.

Overall, the conference was a valuable forum for discussing the latest developments in the finance industry and for sharing new ideas and research results. These conference proceedings provide a valuable resource for academics and practitioners alike, and we hope that they will be a valuable contribution to the field.

December 2022

Jos van Hillegersberg
Jörg Osterrieder
Fethi Rabhi
Abhishta Abhishta
Vijay Marisetty
Xiaohong Huang

Organization

FinanceCom 2022 Conference Co-chairs

Jos van Hillegersberg   University of Twente and JADS.nl,
                               The Netherlands
Fethi Rabhi   University of New South Wales, Australia

FinanceCom 2022 Conference Organizing Chair

Joerg Osterrieder   University of Twente, The Netherlands

FinanceCom 2022 University of Twente - Local Organizing Committee

Xiaohong Huang   University of Twente, The Netherlands
Vijaya Marisetty   University of Twente, The Netherlands
Abhishta Abhishta   University of Twente, The Netherlands

Program Committee

Peter Gomber   Goethe University Frankfurt, Germany
Branka Hadji Misheva   Bern Business School, Switzerland
Jonas Hedman   Copenhagen Business School, Denmark
Ali Hirsa   Columbia University, USA
Ronald Hochreiter   Vienna University of Economics, Austria
Ana Ivanisevic   University of Zagreb, Croatia
Audrius Kabasinkas   Kaunas University of Technology, Lithuania
Ronald Kleverlaan   Utrecht University, The Netherlands
Petre Lameski   University of Ss. Cyril and Methodius, North
                               Macedonia
Bernhard Lutz   Albert Ludwigs University of Freiburg, Germany
Nikolay Mehandjiev   University of Manchester, UK
Dolores Romero Morales   Copenhagen Business School, Denmark
Daniel Tran Pele   Bucharest University of Economic Studies,
                               Romania

Fethi Rabhi	University of New South Wales, Australia
Brahim Saadouni	University of Manchester, UK
Michael Siering	Goethe University Frankfurt, Germany
Nika Šimurina	University of Zagreb, Croatia
Laura Spierdijk	University of Twente, The Netherlands
Vasile Strat	Bucharest University of Economic Studies, Romania
Kristina Sutienne	Kaunas University of Technology, Lithuania
Ekaterina Svetlova	University of Twente, The Netherlands
Claudia Tarantola	University of Pavia, Italy
Ania Zalewska	University of Bath, UK
Sonia Garg	L.M. Thapar School of Management, India
Pradeep Kumar Gupta	L.M. Thapar School of Management, India

Steering Committee for the FinanceCom-Workshop Series

Peter Gomber	Goethe University Frankfurt, Germany
Dennis Kundisch	University of Paderborn, Germany
Nikolay Mehandjiev	University of Manchester, UK
Jan Muntermann	University of Göttingen, Germany
Dirk Neumann	University of Freiburg, Germany
Fethi A. Rabhi	University of New South Wales, Australia
Federico Rajola	Catholic University of Milan, Italy
Ryan Riordan	Smith School of Business, Queen's University, Canada
Christof Weinhardt	Karlsruhe Institute of Technology, Germany

Acknowledgements

Financial support is gratefully acknowledged from the COST (Cooperation in Science and Technology) Action CA19130 Fintech and Artificial Intelligence in Finance, which is supported by COST (European Cooperation in Science and Technology) in the context of the European Commission's Horizon Europe research and innovation framework program.

Furthermore, the editors are grateful to the COST Action CA19130 Fintech and Artificial Intelligence in Finance management committee and working group members for valuable feedback and discussions, as well as all reviewers, authors, and Program Committee members for their extraordinary work on the contents of this volume, and to Springer for their excellent support in producing the FinanceCom 2022 proceedings.

The first two editors are also grateful to ING for the ING - University of Twente joint cooperation on Artificial Intelligence in Finance.

Contents

A Data Analytics Architecture for the Exploratory Analysis
of High-Frequency Market Data 1
  Siu Lung Ng and Fethi Rabhi

Give Them a Second Chance? Prediction of Recurrent Financial
Intermediary Misconduct 17
  Jens Lausen and Benjamin Clapham

A Framework to Measure Corporate Regulatory Exposure 36
  Jascha-Alexander Koch and Peter Gomber

Realising Fair Outcomes from Algorithm-Enabled Decision Systems:
An Exploratory Case Study 52
  Franziska Koefer, Ivo Lemken, and Jan Pauls

The Effect of Changes in Interest Rate Regulation on the Financial
Performance of Banks in Kenya 68
  Jane Ngaruiya, Pat Obi, and David Mathuva

Towards an API Marketplace for an e-Invoicing Ecosystem 82
  Chinmay Manchanda, Walayat Hussain, Latif Rabhi, and Fethi Rabhi

Role of Culture in Customer Acceptance of Neobanks 97
  Koen Meijer, Abhishta Abhishta, and Reinoud Joosten

From Perceived Mobility to the Intention to Use Mobile Payments: The
Role of Positive and Negative Determinants 117
  Petar Dzelalija and Ana Ivanisevic Hernaus

Author Index 133

A Data Analytics Architecture for the Exploratory Analysis of High-Frequency Market Data

Siu Lung Ng(✉) ⓘ and Fethi Rabhi ⓘ

School of Computer Science and Engineering, The University of New South Wales, Sydney,
NSW 2052, Australia
{siu_lung.ng,f.rabhi}@unsw.edu.au

Abstract. The development of cloud computing and database systems has increased the availability of high-frequency market data. An increasing number of researchers and domain experts are interested in analyzing such datasets in an ad-hoc manner. In spite of this, high-frequency data analysis requires a combination of domain knowledge and IT skills due to the need for data standardisation and extensive usage of computational resources. This paper proposes an architecture design for integrating data acquisition, analytics services, and visualisation to reduce the technical challenges for researchers and experts to analyze high-frequency market data. A case study demonstrates how the design can assist experts to invoke different analytics services within a consistent operational environment backed by analytics tools and resources such as a GCP's Big Query running over a Refinitiv Tick History database and a Jupyter notebook.

Keywords: Service Oriented Computing · Data Analytics · High-frequency Data · Jupyter · Refinitiv Tick History · Google Cloud Platform · Big Query

1 Introduction

The availability of high-frequency data has become increasingly important to researchers in fields like econometrics, finance, and accounting. Tick-by-tick data is the most granular high-frequency data that the exchange provides for each tick that the exchange receives from different market participants. The format in which datasets are stored is often suitable for viewing in a spreadsheet. It usually corresponds to a time-stamped event, such as a trade, a change in an instrument's quoted price, an announcement, or a news story. Such datasets require expert knowledge in the relevant domains (such as finance and microeconomics), experience, and IT expertise. Along with identifying necessary data sources and specifying the appropriate search criteria, users must be able to perform a wide range of analytical functions (statistical, data mining, language processing) and display results appropriately (e.g. through visualisations or reports). In general, analysis processes cannot be completely determined in advance since users often perform tasks piecemeal. As they utilize a dataset to build some results, they combine those results to construct other datasets, and the process may be repeated iteratively by applying different search criteria (for example, looking at different time periods or securities of the same product type). Also, users tend to use a variety of tools for storing results and performing routine calculations, such as SPSS, SAS, R and MATLAB. In complex cases, users spend a great deal of time cleaning, reading, converting, and interpreting data, copying results from one file to another, and combining datasets with different semantics, which increases analysis time and error rate.

The scope of our research is to study tools that facilitate the exploratory analysis of high-frequency data by researchers and experts within an organisation. It is becoming more common for organisations to use a combination of cloud-based commercial analytics platforms provided by leading vendors instead of setting up a dedicated analytics infrastructure. In addition, their analysts use popular open-source packages like R and Python to develop custom programs. In the early stages, an analyst uses their domain expertise to analyse data in a trial-and-error fashion, utilising several libraries or software packages. The analysis process involves browsing or visualising specific information from a data source, querying single or multiple data sources, transforming data, identifying patterns, and testing or discovering models. After they are developed and tested, these programs are routinely used to produce reports that can assist executives in making decisions within organisations. However, in an organisation where analytics is not a central focus but an input for everyday decision making, establishing and maintaining a team of data analysts with a mixed-technology infrastructure can end up costing more in the long run than paying high upfront costs for a specialised system.

As it is not feasible for organisations to build bespoke analysis tools; we believe that an architecture based on Service-Oriented Computing (SOC) principles can allow researchers to explore, frame, and solve problems in a technology-independent way [1]. SOC provides an approach for decoupling business processes from specific technology solutions so that users can weave together business services without having to understand the underlying technical implementations. Such an architecture can also leverage the facilities offered by powerful cloud computing platforms which are required when dealing with large datasets, as it is the case with high-frequency financial market data.

The paper is structured as follows. Section 2 reviews the area of high-frequency financial market data analysis and highlights the problem of supporting efficient exploratory data analysis processes. Section 3 describes a solution architecture that is based on the ADAGE framework, which is intended to facilitate the analysis of Refiniv's Tick History database. Section 4 describes a prototype implementation that was carried out for testing and validation purposes. Section 5 concludes this paper.

2 Background

Electronic trading has evolved into a de-verticalized service economy [2]. The increasing use of sophisticated machine learning techniques in pre-trade and post-trade analytics requires more information to be processed to enable faster and more accurate decision-making. Rather than pay for functionality previously provided by investment banks, buy-side companies can now pick and choose their own technology components and trading venues [3]. As a result, the Fintech industry has seen a surge in Small and Medium-sized Enterprises (SMEs) offering software services and component technologies that can perform various functions in the trading cycle [4]. In this paper, we will discuss challenges associated with the analysis of high-frequency data.

As defined by Tsay [5], high-frequency tick data are observations made at daily intervals or on even finer time scales. Market trading transactions are one example. Whenever all transactions are recorded with their associated characteristics, Engle [6] calls this ultra-high-frequency data. Other terms such as "real time tick data" or "tick-by-tick data" have also been used [7]. The "tick" represents one logical unit of information, such as a quote or transaction. Therefore, it is generally accepted that high-frequency data contains intraday observations on financial markets. An important feature of high-frequency tick data is the unequal spacing of data points over time. Most econometric techniques involve analysing data that are evenly spaced over time. Data points arranged regularly are called homogeneous time series, whereas data points arranged irregularly are called inhomogeneous time series [8]. Therefore, a common task in financial time series analysis is transforming inhomogeneous high-frequency time series data into homogeneous time series data. The analysis of high-frequency data is subject to many considerations. If one uses a different interpolation method when generating a homogeneous time series, the results will differ [7]. Using the same set of high-frequency data, users may construct different time series with different criteria (e.g. different interpolation intervals). Allowing domain experts to explore different alternatives when building models is a crucial requirement for any system that supports high-frequency data processing. However, manipulating huge amounts of data without powerful data processing resources presents a challenge to most domain experts.

Obtaining financial market data from a trusted source is another important requirement for a reliable analysis. Due to the high volumes involved, accessing such datasets requires a complex data management infrastructure. There are many providers such as Bloomberg, Alpha Vantage, IEX Cloud and amongst them, Refinitiv which is part of the LSEG (London Stock Exchange Group) is one of the world's largest financial data providers. Refinitiv allows access to intraday trade and quote information for most exchanges and Over The Counter (OTC) markets around the world via its Tick History database which is part of the DataScope product [9]. Most end-users download customized datasets via a web interface according to different search criteria including the type of instrument, exchange, time period, or frequency. Programmatic access to datasets via an API is possible but requires programming skills that are beyond the capabilities of domain experts.

More recently, Refinitiv has partnered with Google and its Cloud Platform (GCP) to provide an alternative to manually collecting high-frequency data [10]. GCP offers a range of cloud services such as a Compute Engine (Virtual machine running in Google Data Centre), Cloud Storage, Cloud SQL (Online relational database services for MySQL and PostgreSQL) and BigQuery (Data warehouse running on serverless infrastructure). In this partnership, Google is promoting the use of BigQuery [11] as a high-frequency financial data processing service. Users can run SQL queries, filter information, and aggregate data through the BigQuery platform to obtain large amounts and high-quality high-frequency market data.

When designing an integrated analytics infrastructure for high-frequency data processing in an enterprise environment, it is essential to satisfy multiple criteria: interoperability, integration, automation, reproducibility, and efficient data handling. Although many tasks can be supported with the use of software tools and cloud computing resources, deploying a pipeline that supports the high-frequency data analysis process is difficult for several reasons. High-frequency data analysis is an evolving field and many skilled software engineers lack the knowledge to build analytics pipelines. Secondly, because of the wide variety of data formats and lack of standardisation in the industry, ensuring information consistency throughout the analysis process can be challenging. Lastly, adapting the infrastructure to frequent changes is very difficult without the involvement of both domain and IT experts which makes it very costly.

As an alternative to being locked in with one particular platform or vendor, there have been attempts at designing systems at a high level of abstraction which would allow multiple technologies to co-exist. For instance, the ADAGE framework [12] is a set of architectural recommendations for the design of analytics applications which leverages the capabilities of SOA and scientific workflow management systems [13]. As part of the ADAGE framework, different types of artifacts such as workflows, services, and data schemas can be modelled with information and instructions about how to utilize them. In this way, an accurate record of the analytics process can be kept and reproduced, which can be useful to keep track of the provenance of results. Furthermore, the framework seeks to be flexible, enabling software developers to utilize the most suitable technologies and components for the development of systems. The capabilities of ADAGE framework to design flexible and adaptable capabilities are illustrated in multiple case studies [12]. Although ADAGE provides a well-developed architecture pattern for designing and developing flexible and maintainable analytics architectures, its limitation is that building modular services that comprise the analytics pipeline is time-consuming and expensive. It is also hard to maintain orchestration with a workflow language. There is no guarantee that a good level of performance can be achieved. With the rise in the popularity of cloud platforms offering powerful data processing services, there is a new opportunity to address this aspect by integrating these services in an analytics pipeline alongside other analytic services provided by end-user tools.

This opportunity is being investigated in this paper through a new architecture based on ADAGE principles which aims at giving domain experts control in the development of high-frequency analytics models using their familiar tools like R and Python whilst the infrastructure leverages heterogeneous software tools and cloud resources in an efficient and seamless way.

3   Proposed Solution

We will present and explain our proposed solution in 5 sub-sections: 3.1 General Principle 3.2 Data Management 3.3 Data Analytics, 3.4 Operation Workflow of Analytics Services and 3.5 Data Visualization.

3.1 General Principles

As mentioned earlier, we leverage the ADAGE framework to propose a solution to support analytics applications for high-frequency financial data. This framework consists of an architecture pattern and associated operational guidelines (see Fig. 1).

ADAGE framework

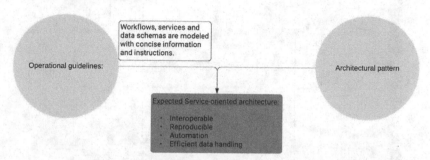

Fig. 1. Components of ADAGE framework

The guidelines state that in order to minimize the development time for ad-hoc analytics activities, integrate analytics services, and simplify analytics operations, several architectural design requirements must be met:

1. Data acquisition is reliable, easy to retrieve, and responsive via a number of *import* services
2. Analytics services are reusable, pluggable, and should be invoked in a consistent way via a number of *transformation services.*
3. The users can download the data in different formats or visualise the outcomes using a graphical user interface via a number of *export services.*
4. The user is in control of the analytics pipeline via *service composition* techniques in a versatile and customizable way.

These principles have been applied to design an architecture for the efficient processing of high-frequency financial data, shown in Fig. 2. This design consists of six layers:

1. The action layer represents what users would do with analytics.
2. The resource layer contains software resources (such as program files, data folders, APIs, etc.) that provide analytics services.
3. The import services layer illustrates what resources are needed for analytics services
4. The proposed platform layer represents the platform and graphical user interface (GUI) that enable the control of analytics services for the users.
5. The transform services layer describes how the imported resources (such as raw datasets) are transformed into outcomes by applying analytics services.

6. The export layer represents the outcomes of the transformation of import resources, such as transforming raw data into the result data by applying analytics services.

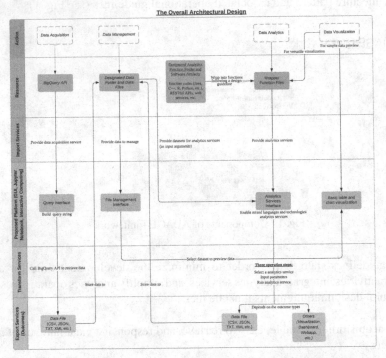

Fig. 2. The overall architectural design of the proposed solution

In the rest of this section, we describe the different aspects of the proposed design.

3.2 Data Management

In the proposed architecture, we used Refinitiv Tick Data database as our market data provider and GCP's BigQuery as a data acquisition tool, respectively. BigQuery provides a web-based application as well as a Python API for data acquisition. Users can create SQL-like query strings and submit them to BigQuery's server to retrieve data. Many analysts and experts in the financial sector are familiar with this data acquisition workflow since SQL is widely used in finance.

In order to facilitate the reuse of data files across analysis services or visualisations, the proposed solution provides an interface to manage data files rather than use another file management application (e.g. Windows File Explorer). Within the same platform which provides data acquisition and analytics services, users can also edit data files (copy, delete, rename, etc.).

3.3 Data Analytics

The ADAGE design principles suggest that analytics functions should be reusable and pluggable, in line with SOA principles. Users should be able to composite a mix of technologies and services to get new analytics services. Instead of using multiple tools to accomplish a series of analytical activities, our solution proposes a "wrap everything into functions" approach for all analytics functions that users can invoke in the same way, which means the analytics services, including APIs and functions compiled with other languages, would be packaged into functions written in a single language. Python is our choice for this solution because it is a versatile language that is easily extensible with other languages such as C/C++, R, Julia, Java, etc. In addition, many popular cloud services, such as Google Cloud Platform, Microsoft Azure, and Amazon AWS, offer analytics services based on Python APIs. Besides, Python itself can be used to develop analytics functions without any involvement of other services.

In order to provide users with the ability to assess different analytics services with the same operational method, wrapper function composition should adhere to a specific guideline. Wrapper functions must specify the types of input arguments and output results (integer, float, string, object, etc.). Figure 3 illustrates an example of writing Python wrapping functions in our proposed solution.

```
def Aggregated_Tick_Data(data: pd.DataFrame=None, time_step:int=5, unit:str='minutes') ->pd.DataFrame:
    calculation = call_R_fucntion_get_aggregation(data, step, unit)
    result = call_Python_function_get_dataframe(calculation)
    return result
```

Fig. 3. Example of wrapper function written in Python.

This is an example of a wrapper function that aggregates tick data into time series data. On line 1 of Fig. 3, there are three input arguments: a pandas-dataframe[1] (pd.Dataframe); an integer (int) indicating the time step; and a string (str) indicating the time unit. The output data type is also a pandas dataframe object (pd.Dataframe). By taking input arguments, this wrapper function first invokes the R function to obtain aggregated values in R-dataframe format (Fig. 3 line 2). The next step is to convert the R-dataframe object into a Python pandas-dataframe object by calling another Python function and finally return the result (Fig. 3 lines 3 and 4). This example illustrates how to integrate data objects and mix language analytics functions/services into a wrapper function. In addition, web-based API services and other data objects can be packaged in the same way.

Furthermore, wrapper functions and analytics programs in other languages should be stored in a designated function file and folder. In order to update or upgrade the analytics services, developers only need to add new wrapper functions in the designated function file and put corresponding programs into the designated function folder.

---

[1] https://pandas.pydata.org/.

3.4   Operation Workflow of Analytics Services

The proposed architecture aims to provide a consistent operating workflow for any kind of analytics service. Figure 4 illustrates the workflow for invoking analytics services in our proposed architecture. The workflow is as simple as the 3 displayed steps. Users must first select an analytics service from a drop-down widget, then input the input parameters via textboxes or other widgets, and finally run the service by clicking a button.

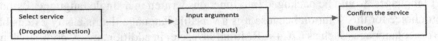

Fig. 4.   The operation workflow for running analytics services in the proposed solution.

3.5   Data Visualisation

The proposed architecture supports any visualization tool as a plugin. There are many Python packages that provide rich visualisation tools for exploratory data analysis. The proposed solution treats visualizations as analytics services like other analysis functions. The developer can connect any visualisation tool by packaging them into wrapper functions. These visualization functions can be invoked as described in Fig. 4. In addition, the proposed solution also provides a standalone interface of basic table and chart visualisation for data preview.

4   Implementation

To demonstrate how our design can facilitate ad-hoc analysis of high-frequency data, we created a program in the Jupyter notebook[2] environment. There are many open-source Python packages that can be used to build interactive user interfaces. We used HoloViews Panel[3] to create the GUI that is able to render the interface on Jupyter notebook cells or HTML browser as a web application. Figure 5 shows the interface overview of the proposed solution.

---

[2] https://jupyter.org/.
[3] https://panel.holoviz.org/index.html.

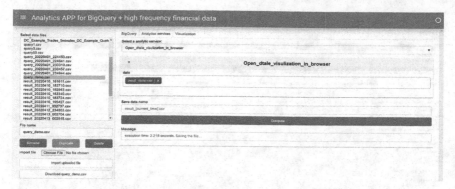

Fig. 5. The interface overview of the proposed solution

The proposed GUI (in proposed platform layer) is divided into two sections. A file management section on the left sidebar lets users manage their data files. The right area section contains several tabs that allow users to switch interfaces for analytics services, BigQuery data acquisition, and data preview visualisation.

4.1 Data Management Section

The data management section's interface is shown in the left sidebar in Fig. 5. It consists of a list control widget showing data files' names and buttons for file management activities. Users can manage datasets by selecting files (in resource layers) from the list widget and by clicking buttons to copy, download, delete, import, or rename files, etc. The data file list will be updated whenever new data files are downloaded from BigQuery or generated by analytics services, making new data files available to other analytics services.

4.2 BigQuery Data Acquisition Section

Figure 6 shows the BigQuery data acquisition interface. This section allows users to access market data through the BigQuery API (in resource layer). To securely enable the BigQuery service with two-factor authentication, users must first upload a credential file to the GUI and then log in to Google Cloud Platform through the pop-up window. With BigQuery enabled, users can create a query string through the GUI and then submit the request to retrieve the relevant market data. The backend program uses the BigQuery API to retrieve the data when the confirm button is clicked. BigQuery usually completes data retrieval in seconds but downloading it into data files such as CSV (in Export Service Layer) takes a slighter longer depending on local computing power. Once the data file appears in the data management area, it can be used for analysis.

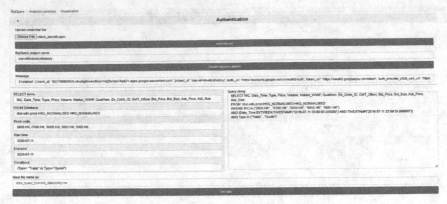

Fig. 6. The BigQuery data acquisition section.

4.3 Data Visualisation Section

Figure 7 shows the interface for the data visualisation section. This section provides users an easy way to preview data as a table or chart (in export service layer). However, it does not meet the requirement of a versatile visualisation tool for ad-hoc analysis of high-frequency data. In our case study, a more comprehensive visualisation tool is defined as an analytics service.

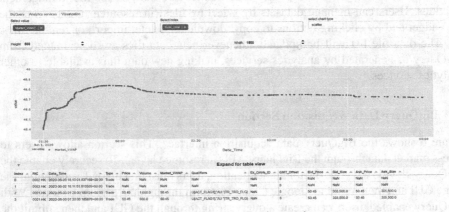

Fig. 7. The data visualisation section

4.4 Analytics Service Section

The analytics service interface is shown in Fig. 8. There is a dropdown control that displays all available wrapper functions stored in the functions file (in resource layer). Users must first select a specific function, and then the program will detect and display the function's parameters and default values, the users can enter the parameters or change the default values in textboxes. In addition, if the parameter data type is recognized as a data object such as a pandas dataframe, the parameter input will display a drop-down widget instead of a textbox; the drop-down list will contain all available data files shown in the data management pane. The interface and data type handling can be automated because all analysis services are defined as Python wrapper functions according to a design guideline mentioned in Sect. 3. Once the compute button is clicked, the analytics service will run and the outcome will be shown (in export layer).

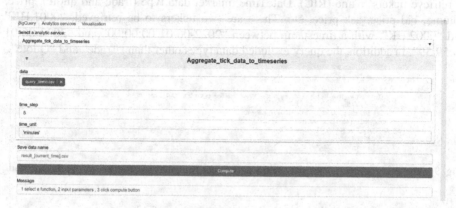

Fig. 8. The analytics service section

5 Case Study

5.1 Case Study Description

A case study was implemented to demonstrate how the proposed solution can be used to analyze high-frequency data. In this scenario, the financial expert needs to obtain the tick data of 2 tickers and then analyze the market spread by aggregating data at different time frequencies (5 and 10 min time steps). The dataset is tick-by-tick trade and quote data of two liquid blue-chip stocks from The Stock Exchange of Hong Kong: 0001.HK and 0002.HK. It consists of total 8127 rows (data points) and 13 columns. The timestep of the dataset is unevenly spaced, and the granularity of the timestep is varying from 1 micro-seconds (10^{-6}) to hundred-seconds (10^2).

The result is line charts that visualize market spreads. In the case study, we tested two methods of implementation:

1. Perform analysis with the proposed solution described in Sect. 4.
2. Perform analysis with a traditional method: obtain data from Refinitiv DataScope and perform analysis and visualisation by calling python codes.

In both methods, the analyses are identical, except that the proposed method integrated analysis functions into a single platform with wrapper functions and GUIs. For data acquisition, the proposed method uses a query string to obtain data from BigQuery while the traditional method uses DataScope. In our evaluation, we compared the two implementation methods based on two criteria: 1. User experience and 2. Performance.

5.2 Services Used for the Case Study

The data was retrieved from the BigQuery API via our Python interface by submitting a query string. Figure 9 shows the query string for retrieving tick data. It tells the BigQuery to retrieve tickers' name (RIC), DateTime, market data type (trade and quote), price, volume, bid price, ask price, etc. There are two tickers to be retrieved, "0001.HK" and "0002.HK", with a timestamp between "2022-06-01 00:00:00" and "2022-06-01 23:59:59". In addition, the query excluded data types other than "Trade" and "Quote".

```
Query string
SELECT RIC, Date_Time, Type, Price, Volume, Market_VWAP, Qualifiers ,Ex_Cntrb_ID, GMT_Offset, Bid_Price, Bid_Size,
Ask_Price, Ask_Size
FROM `dbd-sdlc-prod.HKG_NORMALISED.HKG_NORMALISED`
WHERE RIC in ("0001.HK", "0002.HK")
AND (Date_Time BETWEEN TIMESTAMP("2022-06-01 00:00:00.000000") AND TIMESTAMP("2022-06-01
23:59:59.999999"))
AND Type in ("Trade" , "Quote")
```

Fig. 9. The query string for tick data retrieval through BigQuery API for the proposed method.

The two wrapper functions in the designated function folder are:

1. "Aggregate_tick_data_to_timeseries": This function aggregates tick data into a time series. First, it calls backend R functions to perform the calculation and return an R-dataframe object. The R-dataframe object is then converted into a pandas dataframe object using another python function (see Fig. 3 and Sect. 3.3). The output will be saved as a CSV file in the designated data folder.
2. "Open_Dtale_visulization_in_browser": This function imports D-Tale[4] Packages and applies the D-Tale visualisation tool to the selected dataset. A web-based application will open in the browser for users to visualise the dataset.

5.3 User Experience Evaluation

The complete analysis workflow for the proposed method is as follows:

1. Enable the BigQuery service in the login area on the BigQuery tab (see Fig. 6).
2. Create the query string (see Fig. 9) in the BigQuery tab, then click the "Get Data" button to retrieve the tick data (see Fig. 6).
3. In the data management pane (see the left sidebar in Fig. 5), click the CSV file and then go to the visualisation tab (see Fig. 7) to preview and validate the data.
4. In the analytics tab (see Fig. 8), select "Aggregate_tick_data_to_timeseries" from the dropdown widget. In the parameter inputs section, input the file name just retrieved from BigQuery for "data file", "5" for "time step" and "minutes" for "time unit".

---
[4] https://github.com/man-group/dtale.

5. Click the compute button (see Fig. 8), the program will execute the selected wrapper function taking your parameters. The wrapper function will call backend R and python functions to perform the calculation and format transformation, and then save the result as a CSV file. The result will be displayed in the data management pane.

6. After obtaining the CSV file, go back to analytics tab and select "Open_Dtale_visulization_in_browser" (see Fig. 5). Input the CSV file for the parameter and click the "Compute" button. This analytics service will create a D-Tale EDA tool in a pop-up browser for the selected data file. In the D-Tale application, click on "Visulaize" in the menu and select "chart". In the charting application, select datetime for x-axis and market spread for y-axis, and then select the ticker's name for groups. Figure 10 shows the charts of the market spread for 5 min of aggregation.

7. Repeat steps 4 through 7 again with a different time frequency, this time change parameter "time step" to "10" in step 4.

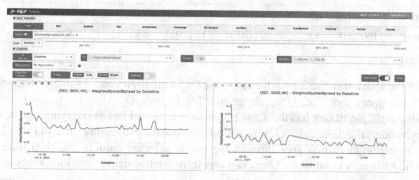

Fig. 10. D-Tale's interactive line charts of the market spread for 5 min of aggregation.

In summary, using our platform, users can retrieve data from BigQuery API with a query string that is familiar to financial experts. The datasets were stored in a destinated folder which does not require extra effort to manage. The data preview visualization tab enables users to validate and preview their datasets before further analysis. During the analysis process, the proposed platform enables users to conduct ad-hoc analyses by invoking two analytics services in a consistent manner, users need only follow three simple steps: 1. choose an analytics service from the dropdown widget, 2. input parameters in the textboxes 3. run the analytics service by clicking a button. In addition, Dtale open-source exploratory data analysis (EDA) visualization tool provides a flexible, zoomable, and interactive chart that is handy for time series analysis in this case study. Compared to the traditional method, the proposed platform provides a simple but versatile analytics functionality for the users, rather than switching between different software tools.

5.4 Performance Evaluation

It takes the same amount of time to perform analytics functions with both methods using the same computing resource and functions. The only difference is the time of operation. To do the analysis with the proposed solution, users need only to invoke analytics services in one platform with a consistent workflow. This could be done within 30 s in our case study. While with the traditional methods, users need to call the analytics functions or use other software to perform analysis and visualization. It would take at least a few minutes depending on the workflow complexity.

We also ran a test to understand BigQuery data retrieval time and bills with different time spans of a dataset. The results were provided by the logging system in BigQuery. Table 1 shows the data retrieval performance result for two different time spans.

Table 1. The data retrieval performance of 3 months and 1-year time spans in BigQuery.

Time span	Ticker	Column	Start time	End time	Process time	Bytes processed/billed
3 months	1606.HK	13	1/1/2020	3/1/2020	3 s	86.56 GB
1 year	1606.HK	13	1/1/2020	1/1/2021	5 s	836.93 GB

For the above test, the 3-month query took 86.56 gigabytes and 3 s to process, while the 1-year query took 836.93 gigabytes and 5 s to process. Also, we found out that querying multiple tickers has the same processing time and bill as querying one ticker, however, querying more data columns would increase the processing time and bill. This is because BigQuery first goes through the whole selected column and then filters it according to query conditions. Users can carefully control data acquisition costs using this information.

5.5 Discussion: Summary of Implementation

Our case study illustrates how the proposed architecture can be used to create an analytics platform to analyze high-frequency market data ad-hoc. The task of aggregating the tick data into time series and visualising it in line charts is a common task for financial analysis. For the data acquisition aspect, retrieving market data using SQL strings is familiar and efficient to financial experts. For the data analysis aspect, the proposed platform provides a simple and consistent workflow for invoking analytics functions. For the visualization aspect, the proposed platform enables a browser-based EDA tool that provides a versatile visualization function that enables users to create different interactive charts with a few button clicks. Furthermore, the proposed program can be rendered on Jupyter Notebook, financial experts can extend or integrate other analyses or financial models in the same Jupyter Notebook. This provides much greater flexibility for ad-hoc exploratory analysis for high-frequency data.

6 Conclusion and Future Work

This study examines the challenges associated with ad-hoc exploratory analysis of high-frequency market data. Traditionally, researchers and domain experts have to use a variety of analytics tools to conduct this type of analysis, resulting in several performance, and code maintenance problems. The proposed solution is an integrated service-oriented architecture that combines data acquisition, analytics, data management, and visualisation into a single user experience. Such an architecture allows the leveraging of cloud resources such as GCP's BigQuery which is used to retrieve high-frequency data from Refinitiv's Tick Data database by using simple SQL-like queries in a very efficient way. It also allows a diversity of analytics services and functions to be plugged into the system. Although all services are packaged as Python functions, the implementation is accompanied by design guidelines that allow developers access to analytics services from a wide range of programming languages and cloud resources in just three operation steps.

The main advantage of the proposed architecture is its openness to a wide range of existing software services and its ability to support automated analytics workflows which can reduce the development time for developers and provide complex analytics at the touch of a button for end-users. However, there are several limitations such as the limited range of analytics services being supported (mainly building intraday time series) and the programming efforts needed when integrating new services. Future work will focus on extending the analytics capabilities of the system and improving the user experience.

The main extension to analytics capabilities being considered will be to include various machine learning functions that are adapted to high-frequency data as this type of data presents many challenges [14]. Supporting real-time analysis of streamed high-frequency market data is another possible extension [15]. In both cases, there will be a need to rethink how to design more advanced wrapper functions and how to manage complex analytics workflows that will result from the application of machine learning processes.

In terms of improving the user experience, there is a need to better leverage the facilities offered by interactive notebook environments like Jupyter. Also, users should be able to use advanced libraries. Finally, the use of AutoML tools [14] to enhance the user experience when performing machine learning tasks will also be investigated.

References

1. Rabhi, F.A., Rana, O.F., Guabtni, A., Benatallah, B.: A user-driven environment for financial market data analysis. In: Kundisch, D., Veit, D.J., Weitzel, T., Weinhardt, C. (eds.) FinanceCom 2008. LNBIP, vol. 23, pp. 64–77. Springer, Heidelberg (2009). https://doi.org/10.1007/978-3-642-01197-9_5
2. Cliff, D., Brown, D., Treleaven, P.: Technology trends in the financial markets: a 2020 vision (2010)
3. Weber, J., Sadlier, M.: Welcome to the new world of equity trade execution: MiFID II, algo wheels and AI (2019)
4. Rabhi, F.A., Mehandjiev, N., Baghdadi, A.: State-of-the-art in applying machine learning to electronic trading. In: Clapham, B., Koch, J.-A. (eds.) FinanceCom 2020. LNBIP, vol. 401, pp. 3–20. Springer, Cham (2020). https://doi.org/10.1007/978-3-030-64466-6_1

5. Tsay, R.S.: Analysis of Financial Time Series. Wiley-Interscience, Hoboken (2005)
6. Engle, R.: The econometrics of ultra-high-frequency data. Econometrica **68**, 1–22 (2000). https://doi.org/10.1111/1468-0262.00091
7. Sun, W., Rachev, S.Z., Fabozzi, F.: Long-range dependence, fractal processes, and in-tra-daily data. In: Seese, D., Weinhardt, C., Schlottmann, F. (eds.) Handbook on Information Technology in Finance, pp. 543–585. Springer, Heidelberg (2008). https://doi.org/10.1007/978-3-540-49487-4_23
8. Dacorogna, M., Gençay, R., Muller, U., Olsen, R., Pictet, O.: An Introduction to High-Frequency Finance (2001)
9. Refinitiv: DataScope Select Data Delivery Platform by Refinitiv. https://www.refinitiv.com/en/products/datascope-select-data-delivery. Accessed 23 May 2022
10. Refinitiv: Refinitiv announces availability of Tick History data on Google Cloud. https://www.refinitiv.com/en/media-center/press-releases/2020/february/availability-of-tick-history-data-on-google-cloud. Accessed 23 May 2022
11. Fernandes, S., Bernardino, J.: What is BigQuery? In: ACM International Conference Proceeding Series, pp. 202–203. ACM (2015)
12. Yao, L., Rabhi, F.A.: Building architectures for data-intensive science using the ADAGE framework. Concurr. Comput. Pract. Exp. **27**, 1188–1206 (2015)
13. Georgakopoulos, D., Papazoglou, M.P.: Overview of service-oriented computing. In: Service-Oriented Computing, pp. 1–28. MIT Press (2008)
14. Ng, S.L., Rabhi, F.A., Whyte, G., Zeng, A.: Introducing the BrewAI AutoML Tool. In: Hussain, W., Jan, M.A. (eds) IoTaaS 2021. Lecture Notes of the Institute for Computer Sciences, Social Informatics and Telecommunications Engineering, vol. 421, pp. 198–207. Springer, Cham (2021). https://doi.org/10.1007/978-3-030-95987-6_14
15. Luong, N.N.T., Milosevic, Z., Berry, A., Rabhi, F.: An open architecture for complex event processing with machine learning. In: 2020 IEEE 24th International Enterprise Distributed Object Computing Conference (EDOC), pp. 51–56 (2020). https://doi.org/10.1109/EDOC49727.2020.00016

Give Them a Second Chance? Prediction of Recurrent Financial Intermediary Misconduct

Jens Lausen[✉] [iD] and Benjamin Clapham [iD]

Goethe University Frankfurt, Frankfurt, Germany
{jens.lausen,benjamin.clapham}@wiwi.uni-frankfurt.de

Abstract. Financial intermediary misconduct represents a major threat for financial markets. Of particular concern is recurrent misconduct, where intermediaries harm investors for their own benefit. This not only impairs affected investors but also decreases trust and participation of investors in financial markets resulting in reduced possibilities for retirement savings and inefficiencies regarding the allocation of funds to the real economy. To solve this societal challenge, recurrent misconduct needs to be prevented. Based on a comprehensive data set, we develop predictive models to identify brokers that repeatedly commit misconduct. In line with existing theories, we show that the disciplinary history of brokers together with the linguistic style and the content of brokers' comments to allegations provide valuable features for predictive models. Our results contribute to the literature on financial misconduct and automated fraud detection. They are valuable for investors and regulators alike assisting them to identify and prevent recurrent financial intermediary misconduct.

Keywords: AI for Societal Challenges · Financial Misconduct · Fraud Detection · Predictive Supervision

1 Introduction

Financial intermediaries such as brokers and financial advisors play a crucial role in the financial system because they enable investors to invest in stocks and other securities by providing market access and investment management [1]. Moreover, financial intermediaries exhibit strong influence on investors' wealth and life planning. Despite their prevalence and importance, large scandals have shaken investors' trust in financial intermediaries [30]. As a consequence, consumers rank financial intermediaries among the least trustworthy professionals and doubt the benefits of the financial system for the economy – a trend, which was fostered by the global financial crisis [31, 45]. Yet, financial intermediaries being at the intersection of investors and financial markets are essential to allocate funds to the real economy. If investors do not trust financial intermediaries and, therefore, do not participate in financial markets, companies and other issuers of stocks and bonds face decreasing supply of liquidity, which endangers the economy. Moreover,

J. van Hillegersberg et al. (Eds.): FinanceCom 2022, LNBIP 467, pp. 17–35, 2023.
https://doi.org/10.1007/978-3-031-31671-5_2

retail investors face reduced possibilities to save for their retirement, which is particularly concerning in the current low interest rate environment. Consequently, innovative solutions are needed to regain investors' trust towards financial intermediaries and the financial system as a whole to solve this highly important societal challenge.

Previous research has already shown that data mining and machine learning techniques can be successfully applied to detect financial misconduct in various domains such as credit card fraud [3] and accounting fraud [40]. However, there is a lack of research on securities fraud and in particular on misconduct by financial intermediaries [29]. Yet, misconduct committed by brokers and investment advisors is particularly concerning since it has significant spillover effects, which result in reduced stock market participation and investments even by those investors that are not directly harmed by intermediary misconduct [15]. Therefore, we add to this research gap by providing new insights to detect recurrent financial intermediary misconduct based on data obtained from BrokerCheck, a comprehensive database providing an easy-to-search disciplinary history for all registered brokers and investment advisors in the US. Data from BrokerCheck has already been used in previous studies to detect intermediaries committing misconduct [24, 32]. However, these studies do not differentiate between those intermediaries with single incidents and those with recurrent misconduct. As in other areas of life, people make mistakes and a misconduct incident in the past, which might also result from an honest mistake, does not necessarily mean that the intermediary will misbehave and harm investors in the future. Consequently, investors should avoid and regulators should detect those intermediaries that repeatedly and purposefully commit misconduct. Therefore, and different from previous studies, we focus on financial intermediaries that had at least one misconduct event in the past and distinguish between those who repeatedly commit misconduct and those who do not. As previous work concludes that information about brokers provided by regulatory authorities is not enough to predict intermediary misconduct [27], we also take the disciplinary history into account and additionally investigate how brokers respond to allegations using natural language processing. Thereby, we are able to identify differences in the way brokers respond to allegations, which might be an indicator for purposeful and repeated misconduct as guided by related theories of deception and criminology. Moreover, we consider whether and how strong financial intermediaries deny the allegations and whether they justify their behavior by attributing it to third parties. According to attribution theory and self-justification theory, such behavior suggests that a person does not see the mistake leading to an incident by herself, and thus, can serve as an indicator for continued misbehavior.

The paper proceeds as follows. First, we describe our research background and elaborate on financial intermediary misconduct and related research on financial fraud detection. We then develop our research hypotheses based on related theories. Next, we describe our data set and the research methodology used to detect recurrent financial intermediary misconduct using different machine learning classifiers. The subsequent section evaluates and discusses the results of our empirical study. Finally, we conclude.

2 Research Background

2.1 Financial Intermediary Misconduct

Misconduct by financial intermediaries refers to the misbehavior of brokers and investment advisors taking advantage of their position as market access provider or investment advisor in order to mislead or exploit clients for their own benefit. This kind of misconduct not only harms those investors who are directly affected but also deteriorates trust in the financial system and reduces financial market participation in general [15]. Yet, misconduct by brokers and investment advisors is relatively common and leads to substantial damages for investors. As an example, the aggregate annual costs of unsuitable investment advice in individual retirement accounts, which is only one facet of intermediary misconduct, amounts to USD 17 billion [6].

Different types of misconduct committed by financial intermediaries exist. One common type of misconduct is the aforementioned unsuitable investment advice. Hereby, brokers and investment advisors urge customers to invest in securities that do not match their risk and return profile but which might lead to higher commissions for the intermediary [7]. Unsuitable investment advice is often, but not necessarily, linked to the misrepresentation of material facts. In case of misrepresentation, brokers and investment advisors deceive customers by providing false or misleading information regarding an investment product with the aim to increase their own revenues [23]. Other types of financial intermediary misconduct such as churning and front running fall under the category securities fraud. A detailed overview of securities fraud and different types of financial market manipulations conducted by intermediaries is provided by Siering, Clapham, Engel, Gomber [34].

Related research on financial intermediary misconduct regularly makes use of data provided by the Financial Industry Regulatory Authority (FINRA) on its website BrokerCheck. FINRA, the responsible competent authority for brokers in the US, mandates the public disclosure of material facts about every intermediary including the disciplinary history of any allegations and wrongdoings [25]. Egan, Matvos, Seru [12] provide detailed descriptive analyses concerning the proportion of intermediaries committing misconduct, the frequency of different types of misconduct, and further broker and firm level statistics. In particular, they conclude that because roughly one third of the intermediaries committing misconduct are repeated offenders, some intermediaries purposefully commit misconduct since this large fraction cannot be explained by bad luck or random complaints by dissatisfied customers. Consequently, intermediaries who repeatedly commit misconduct particularly need to be identified since they constitute a real threat for investors and society's trust in the financial system. Since repeated offenders are especially harmful for investors and the financial system [12], our study develops predictive models using machine learning techniques in order to detect recurrent financial intermediary misconduct.

Concerning the detection of different types of misconduct in financial markets, machine learning classifiers have already been shown to achieve promising results. Since vast amounts of data are generated in financial markets, which also holds for the large number of brokers and investment advisors, manual inspection is time consuming, expensive, and impractical so that the detection of financial misconduct is well suited for machine learning classifiers [42]. In particular, machine learning models have been developed for the detection of credit card fraud [e.g., 3], fraudulent financial statements [e.g., 21], and insurance fraud [e.g., 39].

2.2 Theoretical Background and Research Hypotheses

In order to detect financial intermediaries who repeatedly commit misconduct automatically, we not only rely on the general characteristics of intermediaries provided on BrokerCheck but also add information that previous literature suggests to be meaningful. Specifically, we consider information related to the disciplinary history of each intermediary because research shows that past offenders are significantly more likely to engage in misconduct than the average investment advisor [12]. Moreover, as in lawsuits, financial intermediaries have the possibility to respond to the allegations brought against them. On BrokerCheck, this is solved via public comments in which the broker can provide her own view on the incident by responding to the allegation. Similar to previous literature on machine learning based fraud detection [e.g., 9, 24], we use natural language processing to extract textual features. In addition, we analyze the content of the comments with respect to whether and how strong brokers deny the allegation. Different theories and theoretical models build the theoretical foundation for our feature selection as outlined in the following.

Disciplinary History. As descriptively shown by Egan, Matvos, Seru [12], financial intermediaries with past misconduct events are more likely to repeatedly engage in misconduct. This observation can be explained by Rational Choice Theory (RCT), which is an established theory in criminal science, in particular with respect to white collar crime [5]. RCT claims that criminal and delinquent offenders are reason-ing actors who weigh potential costs and benefits of their crime in order to make a rational decision [5]. Consequently, if multiple offenders are not confronted with rigorous penalties and costs to reimburse clients and, most importantly, do not lose their registration as broker or investment advisor, expected benefits of misconduct will continue to outweigh the expected costs so that dishonest intermediaries do not change their behavior or might even be encouraged in their actions. This is supported by Barnard [2], who rather finds that a pattern of wrongdoing is predictive for recidivism as opposed to an isolated act. Based on a meta-analysis, also Gendreau, Little, Goggin [14] identify the criminal history of offenders as one of the strongest predictors for re-peated wrongdoing. Therefore, we consider features based on the disciplinary history of financial intermediaries besides general information on BrokerCheck in our classi-fiers and hypothesize:

H1: Information based on the disciplinary history of financial intermediaries is valuable to detect financial intermediaries that repeatedly engage in misconduct.

Valuable in this context means that classifiers considering features based on the disciplinary history of financial intermediaries can detect recurrent misconduct better than pure chance. Moreover, these features increase the performance of classifiers that are only based on general intermediary characteristics obtained from BrokerCheck.

Linguistic Style. Concerning the linguistic style, i.e., the way brokers and financial advisors write in their comments to allegations, different theories postulate that the writing of honest individuals differs from those that deceive and commit misconduct. Information Manipulation Theory (IMT) states that deceivers violate four key communication principles inherent to an honest statement [28]. Deceivers tend to present too little or too much information in quantitative terms to conceal or misrepresent information, i.e., they write extremely long or short comments in our context. Moreover, the quality of the information presented is dubious or not relevant to the topic at hand in order to mislead the receiver. Finally, the way in which information is communicated is chosen to be ambiguous. In the context of financial intermediary misconduct, we expect financial intermediaries with recurrent misconduct to make use of these approaches when commenting on the allegations. Scientific Content Analysis (SCAN) [10] is a related theoretical model that considers the style of writing and linguistic features to assess the truth of written statements in the context of criminal investigations. SCAN proposes that, among others, honest individuals write more emotionally and that deceivers differ from truth tellers in how they deny [10]. Since purposefully deceiving individuals differ from honest individuals in their linguistic style, we hypothesize:

H2: Linguistic features of financial intermediaries' comments to allegations are valuable to detect financial intermediaries that repeatedly engage in misconduct.

Denial and Self-Justification. Besides the linguistic style of brokers' comments, we also analyze their content with respect to whether and how strong financial intermediaries deny an allegation and whether they blame others (e.g., their clients, colleagues, or other involved parties) for the incident leading to the misconduct allegation. Attribution Theory (AT) states that humans assign either internal or external reasons for the outcome of an event, while in the latter case, they will not change their behavior in case of negative outcomes [17, 41]. Similarly, Self-Justification Theory (SJT) postulates that when individuals' actions or decisions lead to negative consequences, people tend to defend themselves rather than changing their behavior [37]. If intermediaries that engaged in misconduct do not express the admission of own wrongdoing but strongly deny the allegation or even shift the responsibility to third parties, these intermediaries might not change their behavior but continue to commit misconduct. Consequently, this leads us to our third hypothesis:

H3: Denial and self-justification expressed in financial intermediaries' comments to allegations are valuable features to detect financial intermediaries that repeatedly engage in misconduct.

3 Methodology

In order to develop classifiers to predict recurrent financial intermediary misconduct and to investigate our research hypotheses, we follow the well-established knowledge discovery from databases (KDD) process suggested by Fayyad, Piatetsky-Shapiro, Smyth [13]. This process model proposes a pre-defined structure for data mining problems and is divided into the following steps: (1) data acquisition, (2) feature selection, (3) pre-processing, (4) training, and (5) evaluation. These steps are well suited to develop classifiers based on data that requires substantial pre-processing. Hence, in this section, we describe our approach within each step of the KDD process. We compose our data set based on regulatory data scraped from the website BrokerCheck. We then define several features based on our research hypotheses and derive them from the data set by cleaning and pre-processing the raw data. In a next step, we select appropriate machine learning techniques and compose different classifiers based on the derived features. And last, we evaluate the results of the different classifiers and machine learning techniques with respect to our research hypotheses.

3.1 Data Acquisition

For compiling our target data set, we gather information from the regulatory website BrokerCheck operated by FINRA. BrokerCheck is a comprehensive and easy-to-search database providing information about the background and experience of brokers and investment advisors. It discloses information about the disciplinary history of all brokers and investment advisors that are or have been licensed in the US. BrokerCheck is actively used by investors as indicated by estimated more than 250,000 unique visitors per month. Also, brokerage firms and regulators take into account information from BrokerCheck for hiring and inspection decisions [18]. BrokerCheck discloses general information about each intermediary (e.g., experience, current and past employments, passed exams, and state licenses) and information regarding the disciplinary history of each individual (e.g., customer disputes and regulatory sanctions). Moreover, brokers are able to publicly comment on their past disclosures.

In order to investigate our research hypotheses and to build classifiers to predict recurrent financial intermediary misconduct, we make use of this data by extracting features representing (1) general information of a broker, (2) the disciplinary history, (3) linguistic features based on brokers' comments, and (4) categorial features incorporating different levels of denial and self-justification within brokers' comments. For this purpose, we randomly scrape information from BrokerCheck regarding brokers who had at least one misconduct event in the past. About 7% of financial advisors have a misconduct-related disclosure on their record [18, 24]. To define misconduct, we follow the literature and include all job-related misconduct incidents by using the BrokerCheck categories "Customer Dispute – Settled" and "Customer Dispute – Award/Judgment" [12, 18, 24]. Thereby, we ensure that we only consider job-related categories which represent direct harm to investors. Misconduct-related disclosures, therefore, relate to the actions of brokers that damage individual investors. Customer disputes are mainly based on misbehavior of brokers like misrepresentation, unsuitable recommendations, or securities fraud. We only consider disclosures with a final status (i.e., "Settled", "Award/Judgment") to guarantee that we only include events where brokers admitted wrongdoing/agreed to a settlement or where brokers were convicted. Nevertheless, we consider all other types of disclosures provided on BrokerCheck (e.g., private tax liabilities, liens, and other criminal actions) in the variable "otherDisclosures" because the criminal history of a person also in other areas of life might be of predictive value for intermediary misconduct.

The raw data set consist of 16,206 misconduct cases committed by 9,448 brokers. For our analysis, we consider different points in time of a broker's history, i.e., each date a new misconduct-related disclosure was published. Since all information within the comprehensive BrokerCheck data set is marked with a time stamp, we are able to derive all provided information for a broker at any point in time. For each misconduct event, we check whether a broker commits misconduct within the subsequent ten years or not and assign a corresponding binary label. Hereby, we control for those individuals who stop pursuing business in the field within ten years after a misconduct event (e.g., retired individuals or individuals barred by the authorities) leading to 12,889 observations for our analysis. The binary label (recurrent misconduct or not) is our dependent variable for our supervised learning approach building our prediction models. We select ten years as observation period after a misconduct event as a conservative approach being in line with the maximum amount of years for periods of limitation in US state laws [35]. This approach enables us to exploit our data set to the maximum incorporating a large number of observations representing brokers with recurrent misconduct. Based on these definitions, we derive our features for building our prediction models as described in the next section.

3.2 Feature Selection

In order to leverage the information derived from BrokerCheck for building classifiers to predict recurrent financial intermediary misconduct, we extract a large number of features. To test our research hypotheses, we divide the features into four different categories based on related theories. The first category of features serves as baseline of our analysis and contains features representing general broker information on BrokerCheck (e.g., a broker's experience or her current employment). The second category builds on RCT and brokers' disciplinary history. Therefore, it consists of features describing past misconduct incidents to test H1. Specifically, information regarding past misconduct and non-job-related disclosures, allegations made against a broker, as well as settlement payments are considered. The third category is based on IMT and SCAN and contains different linguistic features of financial intermediaries' comments to allegations to test H2. Last, the fourth category comprises features that build on AT and SJT representing denial and self-justification expressed in financial intermediaries' comments to allegations for testing H3. Table 2 shows all features together with short descriptions.

3.3 Pre-processing

In order to derive our features for the final data set, we need to pre-process our raw data. All features based on information being directly accessible on BrokerCheck (i.e., all features within the general information category as well as the features "misconductCount", "otherDisclosures", "AmountRequested", and "SettlementAmount") do not need any pre-processing and can be directly derived for each observation by aggregating the information. Only for the feature "currentFirm", which is a categorial feature (thus not shown in Table 2) and represents the BrokerCheck identification code of the employing firm, we use one-hot encoding being a standard approach for nominal variables to be processable for machine learning techniques [43].

Regarding the rest of the features in the disciplinary history category, which represent categories for different allegations made against a broker, we apply a multi-step approach. First, we derive different categories of misconduct alleged by customers by manually examining allegations of misconduct-related disclosures. The derived categories (see Table 2) are cross-checked by two researchers. Second, we determine the 100 most common uni- and bigrams based on all allegations to derive a list of search words for each category. Third, we validate the derived word list by applying it to a subset of the allegations and only consider those search words for our final list which enable us to unambiguously assign a certain allegation category. Based on the final word list, allegations are categorized automatically. We apply the same methodology to assign categories to the brokers' comments. For the "denial" category, we additionally control for negating words in order to ensure to capture the correct meaning (e.g., "without admitting", "no wrongdoing").

For analyzing the language brokers use in their comments to allegations in misconduct-related disclosures, we apply common text pre-processing methods and determine quantitative linguistic features. Hereby, we remove parts of the text not containing relevant information such as numbers, abbreviations, single character words, and stop words. We then convert the cleaned text into lower cases and split it into single words. We derive common textual analysis measures reflecting our theoretical background (i.e., IMT and SCAN). Specifically, we include the number of words in the comments to reflect the quantity of information provided by brokers. Moreover, following Zhou, Burgoon, Nunamaker, Twitchell [44], we measure ambiguity in comments by determining the share of complex, modal, and uncertainty words. Thereby, these measures either reflect the quantity or ambiguity dimension of IMT. Based on SCAN, we further include measures for emotional writing such as the share of positive, negative, strong, and emotional words. Moreover, also relying on SCAN, we include the share of negating words as an indication how strong brokers refuse allegations. Even though there exist dictionaries developed for a financial context, e.g., based on financial statements [26], we rely on the more general Harvard IV-4 dictionary because brokers use general and not financial language in their comments. Based on the difference between the number of positive and negative words divided by the sum of the two, we also derive a sentiment score for brokers' comments.

For all observations (i.e., all misconduct incidents), features are derived using the specific point of time for each misconduct incident in a broker's history. Consequently, all broker-related information that occurred or relate to events after the respective misconduct incident are not considered for this observation. Accordingly, for features in the general information category as well as for the features "misconductCount", "otherDisclosures", "AmountRequested", and "SettlementAmount", the broker's information is dated back to the observation's respective time stamp. Furthermore, features representing allegation and comment categories are summed up and linguistic features are averaged for all misconduct-related disclosures until the time stamp of the respective observation. These features indicate how often a certain type of allegation was made, how often the response of a broker indicated a specific level of denial, and which language the broker used on average to comment on allegations based on the current and all previous misconduct events.

We standardize numerical features with zero mean and unit variance. Many machine learning techniques require standardized data since they would estimate larger effects for variables on larger scales. Also, we apply a K-Nearest-Neighbor (K = 50) approach based on all features in our training data to drop outliers with distances above the 99%-percentile to avoid biases in our models [20].

3.4 Machine Learning Techniques and Classifier Configuration

In order to find the optimal model to predict recurrent financial intermediary misconduct, we use different machine learning techniques. In specific, we apply logistic regression (LOG), support vector machine (SVM), random forest (RF), Naïve Bayes (NB), and feed forward artificial neural networks (ANN). These different machine learning techniques generate promising results for different data mining problems [e.g., 9, 19, 21] and especially for financial fraud detection [e.g., 29, 42]. We refer to the literature for technical details of the machine learning techniques [e.g., 11, 16, 20, 38]. In order to avoid overfitted models and to ensure robust and generalizable results, we apply bagging classifiers [4]. We train multiple models by using a random bootstrap sample. We consider 80% of our training data for each single model and determine the classification by a majority vote of all classifiers. We do not use bagging for RF and ANN, since RF classifiers are already a specific kind of bagging classifier and ANNs perform better using the whole training data set.

Table 1. Classifier configuration.

Classifier	General Information	Disciplinary History	Linguistic Style	Denial/Self-Justification
A	X			
B	X	X		
C	X	X	X	
D	X	X	X	X

To analyze our research hypotheses, we use different classifier configurations and compare the results of the classifiers to evaluate whether different feature sets based on the theoretical background and our research hypotheses yield different results, i.e., whether information derived from the features is valuable for classification. We apply all different machine learning techniques as outlined above for each classifier. Table 1 provides an overview of all classifiers. While classifier A is the baseline using only features based on general information on intermediaries provided on BrokerCheck, classifiers B, C, and D additionally use different sets of features based on the disciplinary history of brokers as well as linguistic features and categories representing different levels of denial and self-justification derived from brokers' comments.

3.5 Classifier Training and Evaluation Methodology

For training the different classifiers using each machine learning technique, we use a train-validation-test split making sure to obtain unbiased evaluation results of our models [20]. Hereby, we randomly divide our data set into a training sample, a validation sample, and a testing sample each representing 70%, 20%, and 10% of our data. We train each machine learning technique for all classifiers on the training sample using ten-fold stratified cross-validation in order to avoid overfitting of the models [22] and tune hyperparameters to optimize F1 score based on a grid-search. As described in the previous section, we use bagging classifiers, and thus optimize the number of trained classifiers for each machine learning technique. We then optimize the classification threshold based on the validation set and evaluate the classification performance of the resulting classifiers on the hold-out test sample.

In order to evaluate our classifiers, we rely on different evaluation metrics, which can be derived from the confusion matrix. We compute the common performance metrics accuracy, recall, precision, specificity, and the F1 score to evaluate the performance between different classifiers [36]. Hereby, we consider each performance metric in order to discuss which classifier outperforms the other.

4 Empirical Study

4.1 Descriptive Statistics

Table 2 provides descriptive statistics for the features used to detect recurrent intermediary misconduct separately for cases with recurrent misconduct and those without repeated misconduct within the next ten years. In total, our analysis is based on 12,889 misconduct incidents. Thereof, 6,222 cases (48%) are conducted by repeated offenders leading to an almost equally balanced sample. In addition to the descriptive statistics, Table 2 also shows the results of the Wilcoxon Rank-Sum (WRS) test for equality of means between both groups. These results provide first indications which categories and features show relevant differences between both groups that might be valuable for automated prediction of recurrent financial intermediary misconduct. For most features, we observe significant differences.

Regarding general information on the brokers in our sample, we observe that financial intermediaries that repeatedly engage in misconduct have a significantly longer experience, have worked for more firms, have more exams, and are registered in more states with respective licenses. Looking at the disciplinary history, we also observe that repeated offenders significantly differ in all features from those financial intermediaries that do not engage in another misconduct within the next ten years. In line with Barnard [2], financial intermediaries who repeatedly engage in misconduct show a history of wrongdoings. Specifically, they have significantly more previous misconduct events, which holds for all allegation categories and non-job-related disclosures. Moreover, also the average amount requested by harmed customers as well as the final settlement amount are significantly higher for recidivists, which means that misconduct committed by repeated offenders causes more damage to investors. This again emphasizes the importance to identify recurrent financial intermediary misconduct to retain trust and investor participation in financial markets.

With respect to the linguistic style of financial intermediaries within their comments to allegations, we find that repeated offenders significantly differ from intermediaries without future misconduct for most of the features. As suggested by IMT, financial intermediaries who repeatedly engage in misconduct write shorter comments and use more complex words to mislead the reader [28]. Moreover, they use fewer emotional words, which is in line with SCAN [10].

Concerning the content of brokers' comments with respect to denial and self-justification, we observe significant differences between repeated offenders and financial intermediaries without another misconduct event for all four features. Recidivists significantly more often deny any wrongdoing, more often claim that the case was only settled to avoid potentially higher litigation costs without admitting any misconduct, and more often blame others for the incident leading to investor harm. These observations are in line with AT [17, 41] and SJT [37]. Moreover, financial intermediaries who repeatedly engage in misconduct leave the allegation more often uncommented. Consequently, the descriptive analysis reveals that financial intermediaries with past misconduct events but no future cases and repeated offenders differ significantly regarding general information, disciplinary history, linguistic style, and the level of denial and self-justification providing first descriptive support for our hypotheses H1–H3. Therefore, these features might be valuable for the automated detection of recurrent financial intermediary misconduct using machine learning classifiers.

4.2 Classifier Evaluation

Within this section, we present the results of the different machine learning classifiers applied to detect recurrent financial intermediary misconduct. As described within the methodology section, we consider different classifiers based on varying feature sets in order to investigate our research hypotheses. In the following, we systematically describe the results of the classifiers according to our hypotheses.

H1: Disciplinary History is Valuable to Detect Recurrent Financial Intermediary Misconduct. Table 3 presents the results of our baseline classifier A, which is only based on general information on financial intermediaries, together with the results of classifier B, which additionally takes features based on brokers' disciplinary history into account. Classifiers based on general intermediary information hardly outperform a naïve classification based on random guessing.

The accuracy of classifier A ranges between 56% and 63% (all performance measures are based on the testing data) depending on the machine learning technique used for the classification. In contrast, classifier B, that also takes intermediaries' disciplinary history into account, achieves significantly higher performance metrics compared to classifier A. The best performing machine learning technique using classifier B (RF) achieves a decent accuracy of 70.21% and a relevant recall of 74.92%. These results show that information based on the disciplinary history of financial intermediaries is valuable to detect recurrent misconduct, thus supporting H1.

Table 2. Variable description and descriptives with Wilcoxon rank-sum test for equality of means.

	Feature	Description[a]	Rec. Misc N = 6,222		No Rec. Misc N = 6,667		WRS Test
			Mean	SD	Mean	SD	p
General	experience	The broker's experience in days	3,470	20,371	4,993	3,079	0.00***
	firmsCount	No. of firms the broker was registered	2.91	37	3.67	2.59	0.00***
	examsCount	No. of the broker's passed exams	1.58	12	3.28	1.50	0.00***
	licenseCount	No. of states the broker is licensed to operate business in	4.26	53	1.11	3.97	0.05*
Disciplinary History	misconductCount	No. of misconduct cases (RCT)	18.43	90	1.48	1.83	0.00***
	otherDisclosures	No. of non-job-related cases (RCT)	5.75	14	0.36	0.88	0.00***
	AmtRequested [mn]	Average amount requested from customers in a legal dispute (RCT)	3.14	129.00	0.31	2.56	0.00***
	SettlementAmt [mn]	Average settlement amount (RCT)	8.29	193.75	0.22	3.47	0.00***
	unsuitability	No. of allegations accusing unsuitable recommendations (RCT)	16.58	88	0.55	1.35	0.00***
	misrepresentation	[…] accusing misrepresentation (RCT)	16.89	90	0.59	1.43	0.00***
	negligence	[…] accusing negligence (RCT)	3.63	9	0.29	0.61	0.00***
	unauthorizedTrading	[…] accusing unauthorized trading (RCT)	1.76	6	0.23	0.53	0.00***
	breachFiduciaryDuty	[…] accusing breach of fiduciary duty (RCT)	3.72	11	0.20	0.53	0.00***
	securitiesFraud	[…] accusing securities fraud (RCT)	3.63	58	0.28	0.96	0.00***
Linguistic Style	wordCount	Average number of words (IMT)	269.9	2,521	253.40	303.87	0.00***
	complexWords [%]	Average share of complex words (IMT)	2.89	19.05	3.34	2.39	0.02**
	modalWords [%]	Average share of modal words (IMT)	0.22	3.57	0.12	0.25	0.00***

(*continued*)

Table 2. (*continued*)

Feature	Description[a]	Rec. Misc N = 6,222		No Rec. Misc N = 6,667		WRS Test
		Mean	SD	Mean	SD	p
	uncertaintyWords [%]	Average share of uncertainty words (IMT)	0.33	12.50	0.15	0.40	0.00***
	sentiment	Average sentiment (SCAN)	0.28	1.00	0.00	0.30	0.65
	negativeWords [%]	Average share of negative words (SCAN)	1.92	14.29	2.33	1.94	0.00***
	positiveWords [%]	Average share of positive words (SCAN)	1.90	15.38	2.33	2.04	0.00***
	strongWords [%]	Average share of strong words (SCAN)	2.21	25.00	3.17	2.37	0.00***
	emotionalWords [%]	Average share of emotional words (SCAN)	0.27	4.76	0.18	0.31	0.02**
	negationWords [%]	Average share of negating words	1.13	15.38	0.82	1.37	0.21
Denial/ Self-Justification	denial	No. of comments representing denial of allegations (AT)	11.43	9	0.29	0.63	0.00***
	avoidLitigationCosts	No. of comments claiming to have settled the dispute to avoid uncertain litigation costs (AT/SJT)	5.95	86	0.17	1.14	0.00***
	blameOthers	No. of comments in which the broker blames others (AT/SJT)	0.82	8	0.07	0.31	0.00***
	noComment	No. of misconduct cases where no comment was provided	8.87	46	0.39	0.88	0.00***

Note: * p < 0.1, ** p < 0.05, *** p < 0.01; [a] related theory is provided in parentheses

H2: Linguistic Style Is Valuable to Detect Recurrent Financial Intermediary Misconduct. The results for the classifier additionally taking features based on the linguistic style used by financial intermediaries in their comments to allegations are provided in Table 4.

Compared to classifier B, we observe improvements concerning most performance metrics and machine learning techniques. Again, RF is the best performing machine learning technique leading to the highest accuracy and recall. Consequently, features based on the linguistic style of brokers' comments to allegations are at least marginally

Table 3. Classifier Evaluation H1 (in %).

Feat.	Classifier A					Classifier B				
	General Intermediary Information					Classifier A + Disciplinary History				
Tech.	Acc.	Rec.	Prec.	Spec.	F1	Acc.	Rec.	Prec.	Spec.	F1
LOG	56.56	61.41	54.42	52.02	57.70	69.51	74.28	66.47	65.07	70.16
SVM	56.56	62.86	54.31	50.67	58.27	69.90	73.31	67.26	66.72	70.15
RF	63.38	71.06	60.22	56.22	65.19	70.21	74.92	67.15	65.82	70.82
NB	57.10	62.54	54.87	52.02	58.45	65.79	71.70	62.73	60.27	66.92
ANN	62.06	70.42	58.95	54.27	64.18	69.05	73.31	66.18	65.07	69.57

Table 4. Classifier Evaluation H2 (in %).

Feat.	Classifier C				
	Classifier B + Linguistic Style				
Tech.	Acc.	Rec.	Prec.	Spec.	F1
LOG	69.67	74.28	66.67	65.37	70.27
SVM	69.90	73.79	67.11	66.27	70.29
RF	70.29	75.08	67.19	65.82	70.92
NB	65.71	70.26	62.97	61.47	66.41
ANN	70.05	73.31	67.46	67.02	70.26

valuable to detect recurrent financial intermediary misconduct (H2). Nevertheless, the improvements compared to classifier B are relatively small so that the linguistic features do not substantially improve the predictive performance of classifier C. Given the significant differences in linguistic features for financial intermediaries with and without repeated misconduct (see Table 2), the small performance improvement of classifier C compared to classifier B is surprising at first sight. Due to the fact that a relevant share of misconduct events remains uncommented by the concerned financial intermediary, these principally valuable features are unobserved in a lot of cases, and thus, too few observations are available to significantly improve the performance of classifier C.

H3: Denial and Self-Justification Are Valuable to Detect Recurrent Financial Intermediary Misconduct. Compared to classifier C, classifier D additionally considers features based on the content of the intermediaries' comments reflecting whether and how they deny the allegations and whether they justify themselves by blaming others for the incidents leading to the misconduct. The results of classifier D, which includes all features analyzed in this study, are reported in Table 5. Similar to the previous results, we only see marginal improvements compared to classifier C indicating that features based on brokers' denial and self-justification provide some value for the detection of recurrent financial intermediary misconduct (H3). Given the large and significant differences for features based on denial and self-justification according to the descriptive analysis (see Table 2), again the large share of uncommented misconduct cases seems to limit the ability of these features to increase the predictive performance of the classifier. Nevertheless, the best performing machine learning technique (RF) achieves a decent performance with an accuracy of 70.83% and a recall of 75.56%.

Table 5. Classifier Evaluation H3 (in %).

Feat.	Classifier D				
	Classifier C + Denial and Self-Justification				
Tech.	Acc.	Rec.	Prec.	Spec.	F1
LOG	69.20	72.35	66.67	66.27	69.39
SVM	69.74	73.63	66.96	66.12	70.14
RF	70.83	75.56	67.72	66.42	71.43
NB	65.87	70.26	63.15	61.77	66.51
ANN	69.43	73.79	66.52	65.37	69.97

In addition to assessing one specific configuration of a classifier based on optimizing the classification threshold, we also evaluate our models based on different classification thresholds. Our analyses based on the precision recall curve [33], the receiver operating characteristics curve, and the area under the curve [20] confirm our results. Particularly information retrieved from intermediaries' disciplinary history are valuable to detect recurrent misconduct (H1), whereas features based on the linguistic style as well as denial and self-justification of intermediaries only marginally add value (H2 and H3). Due to space restrictions, the figures are not plotted here.

5 Discussion

Based on different theoretical foundations, we analyze whether information based on the disciplinary history of financial intermediaries, their linguistic style in comments to allegations, and the content of these comments is valuable to detect recurrent financial intermediary misconduct. Our results show that especially the disciplinary history of financial intermediaries is highly valuable for the prediction of recurrent misconduct. Classifiers considering this information significantly outperform a baseline classifier that only takes general information on financial intermediaries into account and which hardly performs better than random guessing (H1). Moreover, our results indicate that also features based on the linguistic style and the content of intermediaries' comments to allegations are valuable for the detection of recurrent intermediary misconduct (H2 and H3).

For all classifiers, RF is the best performing machine learning technique for this particular classification problem. Nevertheless, also the other considered machine learning techniques show decent classification performances for the detection of recurrent financial intermediary misconduct. The best classifier considering all analyzed features achieves a promising classification performance and achieves an accuracy of 70.83% and recall of 75.56%. However, our results indicate that a higher proportion of intermediaries' comments to the allegations might further increase the performance of the classifier. Since the descriptive analysis reveals that repeated offenders and intermediaries without future misconduct significantly differ in their linguistic style, denial, and self-justification, and also since classifiers taking this information into account have a marginally increased performance, brokers' comments appear to be helpful for the prediction of recurrent intermediary misconduct. Therefore, commenting on allegations could be made mandatory for intermediaries or incentives to write comments could be provided to increase the proportion of observations of comment related features and thus the predictive performance of the classifiers. Our proposed classifiers provide a first step to the automated detection of recurrent financial intermediary misconduct. Thereby, our findings contribute to the efforts of preventing intermediary misconduct, which represents a major threat for investor confidence and the financial system.

We are aware of certain limitations. Not all intermediary misconduct events might be included in the data obtained from BrokerCheck. If a financial intermediary committed misconduct in the past but has not been officially accused, no disclosure is reflected on BrokerCheck. Nevertheless, BrokerCheck represents the most comprehensive database of financial intermediary misconduct and is therefore the best data source available. Moreover, financial intermediaries might strategically change their behavior once the classifier is in place. Yet, the most valuable features for the prediction based on the disciplinary history cannot be easily changed. Intermediaries can only stop committing misconduct, in which case the classifier has reached its goal. Still, the proposed classifier should regularly be retrained in order to cope with potential changes in the way intermediaries respond to allegations within their comments.

6 Conclusion

Financial intermediary misconduct represents a major threat for financial markets since it not only directly harms affected investors but decreases trust in the financial system and participation of investors in financial markets in general [15]. Of particular concern is repeated misconduct by single financial intermediaries, which is frequent and where intermediaries purposefully harm investors for their own benefit [12]. Thus, recurrent financial misconduct needs to be detected by regulatory authorities in order to retain trust and investor participation in the financial system.

Based on data obtained from BrokerCheck, a comprehensive database on brokers and financial advisors in the US, we develop classifiers using different machine learning techniques to identify brokers that repeatedly engage in misconduct. In particular, and in line with existing theories, we show that the disciplinary history of brokers as well as the linguistic style and the content of brokers' comments to the allegations provide valuable features for the prediction of recurrent financial intermediary misconduct. The latter two categories, however, only marginally improve the classification performance since not all brokers respond to the allegations so that observations are missing.

With this paper, we contribute to the literature on misconduct in financial markets where previous studies have identified a lack of research [29]. Moreover, we also contribute to the literature on automated misconduct and fraud detection in general by showing the importance to include the disciplinary history for the prediction of repeated offenders. From a practical perspective, our results are relevant for investors, brokerage firms, and regulators alike. Using the proposed classifier, investors are less likely to be harmed by intermediary misconduct. Brokerage firms, that also make use of BrokerCheck information for their hiring decisions [18], can avoid hiring a broker or investment advisor who repeatedly engages in misconduct, which might damage the reputation of the brokerage house. Finally, regulatory authorities can rely on the results of the classifiers to engage in predictive supervision for their random inspections as they do not have sufficient resources to inspect all brokers and investment advisors every year.

Future research could extend our findings to fraud detection in other areas where individuals also have the opportunity to respond to the allegations and where the disciplinary history is visible, e.g., in online marketplaces. Moreover, classifiers for the prediction of recurrent financial intermediary misconduct could be enhanced with associated firm data as previous research has shown that the brokerage house and the coworkers of an intermediary have an influence on her propensity to commit misconduct [8]. In summary, our results show that data analytics based on large and relevant data can be a powerful tool to provide solutions to persistent problems in financial markets and other societal challenges.

References

1. Allen, F., Santomero, A.M.: The theory of financial intermediation. J. Bank. Financ. **21**(11–12), 1461–1485 (1997)
2. Barnard, J.W.: Securities fraud, recidivism, and deterrence. Penn State Law Rev. **113**(1), 189–228 (2009)
3. Bhattacharyya, S., Jha, S., Tharakunnel, K., et al.: Data mining for credit card fraud. A comparative study. Decis. Support Syst. **50**(3), 602–613 (2011)
4. Breiman, L.: Bagging predictors. Mach. Learn. **24**(2), 123–140 (1996)
5. Cornish, D.B., Clarke, R.V.: The Reasoning Criminal: Rational Choice Perspectives on Offending. Springer, New York, NY (1986)
6. Council of Economic Advisors (2015) The Effects of Conflicted Investment Advice on Retirements Savings. https://permanent.access.gpo.gov/gpo55500/cea_coi_report_final.pdf. Accessed 16 Nov 2022
7. Cumming, D., Johan, S., Li, D.: Exchange trading rules and stock market liquidity. J. Financ. Econ. **99**(3), 651–671 (2011)
8. Dimmock, S.G., Gerken, W.C., Graham, N.P.: Is fraud contagious? Coworker influence on misconduct by financial advisors. J. Financ. **73**(3), 1417–1450 (2018)
9. Dong, W., Liao, S., Zhang, Z.: Leveraging financial social media data for corporate fraud detection. J. Manag. Inf. Syst. **35**(2), 461–487 (2018)
10. Driscoll, L.N.: A validity assessment of written statements from suspects in criminal investigations using the scan technique. Police Stud. **17**(4), 77–88 (1994)

11. Duda, R.O., Hart, P.E., Stork, D.G.: Pattern Classification, 2nd edn. Wiley-Interscience, New York, NY (2012)
12. Egan, M., Matvos, G., Seru, A.: The market for financial adviser misconduct. J. Polit. Econ. **127**(1), 233–295 (2019)
13. Fayyad, U., Piatetsky-Shapiro, G., Smyth, P.: From data mining to knowledge discovery in databases. AI Mag. **17**(3), 37–54 (1996)
14. Gendreau, P., Little, T., Goggin, C.: A meta-analysis of the predictors of adult offender recidivism: what works! Criminology **34**(4), 575–608 (1996)
15. Gurun, U.G., Stoffman, N., Yonker, S.E.: Trust busting: the effect of fraud on investor behavior. Rev. Financ. Stud. **31**(4), 1341–1376 (2018)
16. Han, J., Kamber, M.: Data Mining. Concepts and Techniques, 2nd ed. The Morgan Kaufmann Series in Data Management Systems. Elsevier, Amsterdam (2006)
17. Heider, F.: The Psychology of Interpersonal Relations. John Wiley & Sons Inc., Hoboken, NJ (1958)
18. Honigsberg, C., Jacob, M.: Deleting misconduct: the expungement of brokercheck records. J. Financ. Econ. **139**(3), 800–831 (2021)
19. Humpherys, S.L., Moffitt, K.C., Burns, M.B., et al.: Identification of fraudulent financial statements using linguistic credibility analysis. Decis. Support Syst. **50**(3), 585–594 (2011)
20. James, G., Witten, D., Hastie, T., et al.: An Introduction to Statistical Learning. With Applications in R. Springer Texts in Statistics. Springer, New York, Heidelberg, Dordrecht, London (2017). https://doi.org/10.1007/978-1-4614-7138-7
21. Kirkos, E., Spathis, C., Manolopoulos, Y.: Data mining techniques for the detection of fraudulent financial statements. Expert Syst. Appl. **32**(4), 995–1003 (2007)
22. Kohavi, R.: A study of cross-validation and bootstrap for accuracy estimation and model selection. In: Proceedings of the 14th International Joint Conference on Artificial Intelligence, pp. 1137–1143 (1995)
23. Krausz, M., Paroush, J.: Financial advising in the presence of conflict of interests. J. Econ. Bus. **54**(1), 55–71 (2002)
24. Lausen, J., Clapham, B., Siering, M., et al.: Who is the next wolf of wall street? Detection of financial intermediary misconduct. J. Assoc. Inf. Syst. **21**(5), 1153–1190 (2020)
25. Lazaro, C.: Has expungement broken brokercheck? J. Bus. Secur. Law **14**(2), 125–150 (2014)
26. Loughran, T., McDonald, B.: When is a liability not a liability? Textual analysis, dictionaries, and 10-Ks. J. Financ. **66**(1), 35–65 (2011)
27. McCann, C., Qin, C., Yan, M.: How widespread and predictable is stock broker misconduct? J. Invest. **26**(2), 6–25 (2017)
28. McCornack, S.A.: Information manipulation theory. Commun. Monogr. **59**(1), 1–16 (1992)
29. Ngai, E., Hu, Y., Wong, Y.H., et al.: The application of data mining techniques in financial fraud detection. A classification framework and an academic review of literature. Decis. Support Syst. **50**(3), 559–569 (2011)
30. Palazzo, G., Rethel, L.: Conflicts of interest in financial intermediation. J. Bus. Ethics **81**(1), 193–207 (2008)
31. Prior, A.: Brokers Are Trusted Less Than Uber Drivers, Survey Finds (2015). https://www.wsj.com/articles/brokers-are-trusted-less-than-uber-drivers-survey-finds-1438081201. Accessed 16 Nov 2022
32. Saito, T., Rehmsmeier, M.: The precision-recall plot is more informative than the ROC plot when evaluating binary classifiers on imbalanced datasets. PLoS ONE **10**(3), 1–21 (e0118432) (2015)
33. Siering, M., Clapham, B., Engel, O., et al.: A taxonomy of financial market manipulations. Establishing trust and market integrity in the financialized economy through automated fraud detection. J. Inf. Technol. **32**(3), 251–269 (2017)

34. Silver Law Group (2016) What is the Statute of Limitations on Securities Fraud? https://www.silverlaw.com/blog/statute-limitations-securities-fraud/. Accessed 16 Nov 2022

35. Sokolova, M., Lapalme, G.: A systematic analysis of performance measures for classification tasks. Inf. Process. Manag. **45**(4), 427–437 (2009)

36. Staw, B.M.: Knee-deep in the big muddy: a study of escalating commitment to a chosen course of action. Organ. Behav. Hum. Perform. **16**(1), 27–44 (1976)

37. Vapnik, V.N.: Statistical Learning Theory. Wiley, New York, NY (1998)

38. Viaene, S., Dedene, G., Derrig, R.: Auto claim fraud detection using Bayesian learning neural networks. Expert Syst. Appl. **29**(3), 653–666 (2005)

39. Wang, S.: A comprehensive survey of data mining-based accounting-fraud detection research. In: International Conference on Intelligent Computation Technology and Automation, pp. 50–53 (2010)

40. Weiner, B.: An attributional theory of achievement motivation and emotion. Psychol. Rev. **94**(4), 548–573 (1985)

41. West, J., Bhattacharya, M.: Intelligent financial fraud detection. A comprehensive review. Comput. Secur. **57**, 47–66 (2016)

42. Wooldridge, J.M.: Introductory Econometrics. A Modern Approach, 4th ed. ISE - International Student Edition. South-Western Cengage Learning, Mason, OH (2009)

43. Zhou, L., Burgoon, J.K., Nunamaker, J.F., et al.: Automating linguistics-based cues for detecting deception in text-based asynchronous computer-mediated communications. Group Decis. Negot. **13**(1), 81–106 (2004)

44. Zingales, L.: Presidential address: does finance benefit society? J. Financ. **70**(4), 1327–1363 (2015)

A Framework to Measure Corporate Regulatory Exposure

Jascha-Alexander Koch[1]([⊠]) [iD] and Peter Gomber[2] [iD]

[1] University of Siegen, Siegen, Germany
jascha-alexander.koch@uni-siegen.de
[2] Goethe University Frankfurt, Frankfurt am Main, Germany
gomber@wiwi.uni-frankfurt.de

Abstract. The amendment of existing and the passing of new regulations keep the corpus of regulation changing and growing dynamically. Against this background, companies face increasing costs to comply with existing and upcoming regulation. However, the high amount of regulatory texts makes it difficult for companies to identify which regulations apply to them. While regulatory technology, so-called RegTech, enables companies to comply with regulatory requirements or serves supervisory authorities to check compliance, there are no tools that enable companies to efficiently determine the relevance of a regulation in an automated manner. Therefore, this paper develops a decision support framework that makes use of techniques from natural language processing. We apply our approach to the Code of Federal Regulations in the U.S and discuss the results. As a key practical implication, our framework enables companies to retrieve regulations that speak to their business activities and may require compliance actions.

Keywords: RegTech · Regulatory Exposure · Code of Federal Regulations · Language Processing

1 Introduction

In the last decades, policy makers have aimed to design a regulatory framework that fosters a safe and resilient economic system and society. Regulating economic entities is necessary, but the optimal amount of regulation and optimal level of complexity are subject of an intense debate [2, 13]. Particularly in recent years, companies are confronted with an increasing amount of regulation they have to comply with [8]. Complying with a regulation is only possible if companies identify ex ante the set of regulations that are relevant to them which is increasingly difficult given the dynamic growth of amendments of existing and the passing of new regulations.

Against this background, we investigate how regulatory technology (RegTech) can help firms to identify relevant regulations in an automated way distinguishing between applicable and non-applicable legal texts. More specifically, we introduce a framework that relies on natural language processing (NLP) techniques to investigate the relevance of a legal act for a company's activities (its services and products).

J. van Hillegersberg et al. (Eds.): FinanceCom 2022, LNBIP 467, pp. 36–51, 2023.
https://doi.org/10.1007/978-3-031-31671-5_3

Previous research has suggested several approaches to measure firms' exposure to regulation. However, these approaches largely ignore firms' characteristics, like their specific business activities. Research has mainly focused on either a firm's exposure to regulation at the industry level [1], aggregate macroeconomic level [4], or at the firm level as implied by the burden of paperwork [7]. Paperwork in [7] refers to information companies have to provide to regulatory authorities in the U.S. and the compliance burden can be measured, e.g., by the number of hours needed to collect all relevant information necessary to fulfill the respective regulatory requirement. However, these approaches tend to produce biased results because firms often do not operate in just one specific static industry but dynamically in several industries [e.g., 6] and regulatory exposure concerning new regulations (ex-ante view) cannot be measured by the burden of paperwork regarding already covered regulatory requirements (ex-post view). To overcome these shortcomings, we introduce a novel framework that maps self-disclosed information, in which firms qualitatively describe their business activities, to legal acts that may affect the respective firms. We rely on firms' disclosed narrative view regarding their own business activities and calculate how likely it is that a certain legal act is relevant for them.

With our approach we contribute to the theoretical understanding of whether firms' disclosed self-image allows for drawing conclusions on firms' regulatory exposure, i.e., how likely it is that a specific regulation applies to the firm under consideration. From a practical perspective, we contribute to the development of a new RegTech approach that shall help firms to efficiently and automatically assess upcoming or changing regulation in a timely manner. Our framework can be applied in a decision support system to assess the relevance of a regulation for a company's business and to enable humans to focus on these pre-assessed regulations instead of manually inspecting all texts. We evaluate our approach by applying it to the U.S. Code of Federal Regulation (CFR) and find that our framework provides a solid fundament for evaluating firms' regulatory exposure.

This paper is structured as follows. In Sect. 2, we present our research background. In Sect. 3, we introduce our framework to measure firm-specific exposure to regulation (Sect. 3.1), and we describe the data used for the application of our framework (Sect. 3.2). In Sect. 4, we present the results of the application of our framework (Sect. 4.1) and the evaluation of these results (Sect. 4.2). Finally, Sect. 5 concludes.

2 Research Background

Firms have to inform themselves about regulatory changes and new regulatory initiatives in all countries they operate. It is common knowledge that such regulations have a significant effect on businesses [e.g., 9], their productivity [e.g., 11], and innovation processes [e.g., 12]. As a consequence, academic research has investigated the broader relationship between regulation and economy and, more specifically, how to measure regulatory exposure.

For instance, [4] investigate the relationship between federal regulation and the U.S. economy. They focus on the aggregate macroeconomic level and do not consider any firm-specific characteristics showing that growth in regulation impedes economic growth and productivity. However, one important foundation to clarify the effect of regulation on firms is to determine which kind of firms are affected by a specific legal act in particular. Looking at the economy in general does not enable to make detailed statements about individual firms. [1] go a step further and introduce "RegData" – which "measures regulation for industries at the two, three, and four-digit levels of the North American Industry Classification System" (p. 109). With this approach, the authors consider industry-specific characteristics but ignore firm-specific characteristics, e.g., product portfolios, and measure regulatory exposure only at the overall industry level. As a consequence, two firms of a certain industry will be described by the same regulatory exposure although they might have different business models or products and services. [7] is the first to measure regulatory exposure at the firm level. To do so, he focuses on regulatory paperwork that has to be done by firms and empirically finds that higher regulatory intensity corresponds to lower capital investment and less new hires by firms. The mapping from the industry level to the firm level is based on industry-specific revenues. However, paperwork does not allow for quantifying firms' regulatory exposure and for judging which regulation a firm has to comply with. Moreover, this approach is only sensible ex post, i.e., when regulations are already passed and have already led to paperwork. Thus, based on this approach, firms are not able to investigate their regulatory exposure concerning new legal acts that will be applied in the future. To overcome these shortcomings, we introduce a novel framework that operates at the firm level, is not dependent on economic figures, and also serves to evaluate upcoming regulations (ex-ante perspective).

3 Measuring Regulatory Exposure

3.1 Measurement Framework

Firms describe their activities, i.e., products and services, in their annual reports in textual form. These descriptions serve as starting point for setting up our framework to measure regulatory exposure. For identifying applicable regulatory documents, we consider digitally readable files of legal acts to enable automatic processing. Then, we compute the textual similarity between a firm's (self-disclosed) business description and the respective regulatory documents to obtain a measure of firm-specific regulatory exposure. Regulatory exposure measures the extent to which a company is affected by a legal act.

To compute this similarity score, we apply several preprocessing steps to data at hand to arrive at a reasonable and meaningful representation of both the business descriptions and legal texts:

First, for the preprocessing of firms' self-disclosed business descriptions, we follow [6] and select only nouns (i.e., common nouns) and proper nouns (i.e., nouns that refer to unique entities, like names) from firm' business descriptions using a parts-of-speech (POS) tagger. Then, we remove geographical names and terms that appear in more than 25% of all documents [see 6]. Further, we require that a noun has to appear in the business descriptions of at least five firms and delete all nouns that appear in less than five documents to reduce noise resulting from unimportant and too specific terms at the firm level. We run these steps to gauge those words that are most likely to reflect firms' products and services. After manual checks, we conclude that words other than nouns, e.g., adjectives, refer mostly to more common words that are not product- or service-specific. We consider unigrams but also concatenate subsequent words to noun n-grams. For instance, the term "distribution facility" refers to one meaning unit and, instead of using "distribution" and "facility" separately, we use the bigram "distribution facility". Finally, we lemmatize nouns and remove words that consist of only one letter.

Second, regarding the preprocessing of regulatory documents, we divide the entirety of documents in logical sections. More specifically, we follow the given structure of the documents (e.g., legal paragraphs). Then, for each legal paragraph (e.g., Title 1 Chapter 2 Part 40) in the regulatory documents, we extract the set of nouns contained in the respective text. Here, we only keep the set of nouns as identified in firms' business descriptions (see above) to make sure that we only keep textual content of the legal paragraphs that is related to companies' products and services. In other words, nouns and proper nouns from the regulatory texts are only kept if they are related to the list of nouns extracted from business descriptions of one particular year. In this regard, we also accept synonyms and related words – the nouns do not have to appear identically but we allow for both contextually and semantically similar nouns. For considering synonyms and related words, we rely on a pre-trained word-to-vector model[1] that returns a list of related nouns for each noun. This step is important to guarantee a better fit between the nouns extracted from the business descriptions and the legal paragraphs.

Based on these two main steps of preprocessing for both companies' business descriptions and legal paragraphs, we measure the level of regulatory exposure of firm i in year t to each legal paragraph c. We do so by calculating the Jaccard similarity between $N_{i,t}$ and $N_{c,t}$, i.e.,

$$J(i, c, t) = \frac{N_{i,t} \cap N_{c,t}}{N_{i,t} \cup N_{c,t}} \tag{1}$$

where $N_{i,t}$ is the list of unique nouns of the business description of firm i and $N_{c,t}$ for legal paragraph c in year t. We only consider the appearance of nouns and do not focus on nouns' frequency since the frequency of nouns is highly dependent on the way texts are written and, thus, biased by the writing style. For example, if a company keeps a product specification short in the business description they are not less subject to a certain law – and also short and concise legal paragraphs might not be less relevant for firms. We reduce this potential bias by focusing on nouns' unique appearance.

The Jaccard similarity as expressed in Eq. (1) ranges in the interval between 0 and 1 and can be interpreted as a quantification of the regulatory exposure of firm i to the legal paragraph c in year t. More specifically, the higher the Jaccard similarity, the higher is a firm's regulatory exposure to the respective legal paragraph.

This framework allows for a firm-specific evaluation of exposure to a specific legal text and is independent from economic characteristics of a firm. Moreover, our approach allows for an ex-ante analysis across (newly passed) legal documents.

---

[1] We use the sense2vec model: https://github.com/explosion/sense2vec#pretrained-vectors.

3.2 Application to U.S. Data

To apply our framework, we focus on the U.S. because both business descriptions and legal documents are digitally accessible and easily available there and have been used in several prior research studies [e.g., 1].

As a source of legal documents, we use the U.S. Code of Federal Regulations (CFR), which contains the most relevant collection of legal texts in the U.S. at the federal level besides the U.S. Code. The CFR is structured by Titles (1 to 50), Chapters, and Parts. Based on the CFR, we measure the extent to which firms are affected by a regulation, i.e., the legal text at the Title-Chapter-Part level. We download yearly snapshots of the CFR from 1999 until 2019[2]. The CFR comprises the general and permanent regulations in the U.S., but not every public law becomes part of the CFR. The entry of laws into the CFR depends on the decision of the Office of the Law Revision Counsel (OLRC). We focus on the information in the CFR at the Title-Chapter-Part level. A representative example of the XML-based CFR text – as used for our application – is provided in Fig. 1. This figure shows the beginning of Title 12 Chapter 5 Part 56 in the CFR in 2019. The elements provided in <...> are part of the XML structure and enable automated processing. For extracting the nouns, only the proper text in these structures is considered.

```
- <SECTION>
    <SECTNO>§ 5.56</SECTNO>
    <SUBJECT>Inclusion of subordinated debt securities and mandatorily redeemable preferred stock as Federal savings association
      supplementary (tier 2) capital.</SUBJECT>
  - <P>
      (a)
      <E T="03">Scope and definitions.</E>
      (1) A Federal savings association must comply with this section in order to include subordinated debt securities or mandatorily
      redeemable preferred stock ("covered securities") in tier 2 capital under 12 CFR 3.20(d) and to prepay covered securities
      included in tier 2 capital. A savings association that does not include covered securities in tier 2 capital is not required to
      comply with this section. Covered securities not included in tier 2 capital are subject to the requirements of § 163.80 of this
      chapter.
      <PRTPAGE P="390"/>
    </P>
    <P>(2) For purposes of this section, mandatorily redeemable preferred stock means mandatorily redeemable preferred stock that
      was issued before July 23, 1985 or issued pursuant to regulations and memoranda of the Federal Home Loan Bank Board and
      approved in writing by the Federal Savings and Loan Insurance Corporation for inclusion as regulatory capital before or after
      issuance.</P>
  - <P>
      (b)
      <E T="03">Application and notice procedures</E>
      —(1)
      <E T="03">Application or notice to include covered securities in tier 2 capital</E>
      —(i)
      <E T="03">Application.</E>
      Unless a Federal savings association is an eligible savings association filing a notice under paragraph (b)(1)(ii) of this section,
      it must file an application seeking the OCC's approval of the inclusion of covered securities in tier 2 capital. The savings
      association may file its application before or after it issues covered securities, but may not include covered securities in tier 2
      capital until the OCC approves the application.
    </P>
```

Fig. 1. Example: XML-based CFR, Title 12 Chapter 5 Part 56, 2019 (excerpt). (https://www.gov info.gov/bulkdata/CFR/2019/title-12/CFR-2019-title12-vol1.xml.)

In order to have a time-varying representation of products and services of listed firms in the U.S., we rely on the "Item 1. Business Descriptions" in their annual reports they file with the Securities and Exchange Commission (SEC), i.e., form 10-K. We use these business descriptions as a proxy for companies' self-disclosed narratives on their business activities. These business descriptions disclosed in textual form have been used widely in prior literature to derive a granular characterization of firms' business activities [e.g., 5, 6]. We downloaded firms' 10-K, 10-K405, 10KSB, and 10KSB40 filings

---

[2] The historical versions of the U.S. Code of Federal Regulation provided in the XML format are available at: https://www.govinfo.gov/bulkdata/CFR.

PART I

ITEM 1. BUSINESS

Overview

    JPMorgan Chase & Co. ("JPMorgan Chase" or the "Firm", NYSE: JPM), a **financial holding company** incorporated under Delaware law in 1968, is a leading global **financial services** firm and one of the largest **banking institutions** in the United States of America ("U.S."), with operations worldwide; JPMorgan Chase had $2.6 trillion in assets and $256.5 billion in stockholders' equity as of December 31, 2018. The Firm is a leader in **investment banking, financial services** for consumers and small businesses, **commercial banking, financial transaction processing** and asset management. Under the J.P. Morgan and Chase brands, the Firm serves millions of customers in the U.S. and globally many of the world's most prominent corporate, institutional and government clients.

    JPMorgan Chase's principal **bank subsidiaries** are JPMorgan Chase Bank, National Association ("JPMorgan Chase Bank, N.A."), a national **banking association** with U.S. branches in 27 states and the District of Columbia as of December 31, 2018, and Chase Bank USA, National Association ("Chase Bank USA, N.A."), a national **banking association** that is the Firm's principal **credit card**-issuing bank. In January 2019, the OCC approved an application of merger which was filed by JPMorgan Chase Bank, N.A. and Chase Bank USA, N.A. in December 2018 and which contemplates that Chase Bank USA, N.A. will merge with and into JPMorgan Chase Bank, N.A., with JPMorgan Chase Bank, N.A. as the surviving **bank**. For additional information refer to Supervision and Regulation on pages 1-6 in the 2018 Form 10-K. JPMorgan Chase's principal **nonbank subsidiary** is J.P. Morgan Securities LLC ("J.P. Morgan Securities"), a U.S. **broker-dealer**. The bank and **non-bank subsidiaries** of JPMorgan Chase operate nationally as well as through overseas branches and subsidiaries, representative offices and subsidiary foreign banks. The Firm's principal operating subsidiary in the U.K. is J.P. Morgan Securities plc, a subsidiary of JPMorgan Chase Bank, N.A.

... (excerpt)

Fig. 2. Example: 10-K filing of JP Morgan Chase, Business Description, Fiscal Year 2018. (https://www.sec.gov/ix?doc=/Archives/edgar/data/0000019617/000001961719000054/corp10 k2018.htm.)

(subsequently subsumed under "10-K filings") from the SEC website using information from quarterly index files.[3] For each company, we consider only the 10-K filings that include the business description. We automatically extracted valid business descriptions from 105,698 out of originally 115,935 10-K filings from 1994 until 2019 via an algorithm that relies on regular expressions. Older files increasingly exhibit non-standardized, heterogeneous, and noisy document structures (such as typos, erroneous or non-existent tables of contents, non-XBRL formatting, etc.). Therefore, we adjusted the algorithm iteratively after manual inspections to eliminate the extraction of false or missing business descriptions. However, the structure of the remaining 10-K filings is too specific to extract the descriptions without manually analyzing each file. Consequently, we discarded erroneous files to avoid biases and distorted results. All correctly processed files are used for the application of our framework. An example of an extracted business description from 10-K filings is provided in Fig. 2 (relevant nouns with a financial context are highlighted).

---

[3] The quarterly index files for electronic retrieval system for SEC filings (EDGAR) are available at: https://www.sec.gov/Archives/edgar/full-index/.

4   Results and Evaluation

4.1   Results of Application to CFR

After preparing the CFR documents and the business descriptions from companies' 10-K filings, we apply the framework as described in Sect. 3.1. First, we extract nouns and proper nouns of the business descriptions and, then, nouns and proper nouns from the CFR Title-Chapter-Parts (hereafter: "Title-Parts") for each year. As an important step of data preprocessing, we only keep those nouns and proper nouns from the CFR documents that appear at least once in the firms' business descriptions (see Sect. 3.1). This helps to reduce noise due to nouns in the CFR that are unrelated to companies' products and services, and are likely to bias our results. In Fig. 3, we show an example for this step of preprocessing presented by word clouds that highlight those nouns that are most present in the respective sets. As an example, we have chosen the Truth in Savings Act, Title 12 Part 1030 of the CFR, which has the purpose to "enable consumers to make informed decisions about accounts at depository institutions" [3], e.g., by the clear and uniform disclosure of annual percentage yields. On the left in Fig. 3, we show the nouns before the preprocessing step – and, on the right, after the preprocessing. It is apparent that those nouns (e.g., institution, interest, account) have disappeared, which are less likely to be characteristic for the linkage between legal texts and firms' business activities because these nouns tend to be rather general. In the right plot of Fig. 3, one can see that nouns like percentage yield, interest rate, or deposit stand out and are rather specific to the act itself.

Fig. 3. Word clouds of all nouns (left) and preprocessed nouns (right) of Title 12 Part 1030.

These preprocessing steps enable us to compare the textual content of a specific Title-Part with each firm's business description and to compute a firm's regulatory exposure in a particular year. We calculate for each firm in our sample its regulatory exposure for each Title-Part in the CFR (i.e., for all Parts of Titles 1 – 50) on a yearly basis. Table 1 presents an extraction of the overall result table containing all company and Title-Part combinations. Specifically, the table shows Title 12 Part 1030 for four exemplary companies and different years. The two financial institutions, presented in the table, Southern Missouri Bancorp, Inc. and United Bancshares, Inc., reveal higher regulatory exposure to the Truth in Savings Act than the two other companies, Starrett L S Co. and Rockwell Automation, Inc., across all years in the period from 2016 until 2019.

The resulting data does not only allow for static snapshots of company and legal code combinations – instead, it is possible to track changes in firms' regulatory exposure over

Table 1. Result Matrix of Firms' Regulatory Exposure.

Company	Year	Reg. Exposure Title ... Part ...	Reg. Exposure Title 12 Part 1030
SOUTHERN MISSOURI BANCORP, INC	2016	...	0.0818
SOUTHERN MISSOURI BANCORP, INC	2017	...	0.0824
SOUTHERN MISSOURI BANCORP, INC	2018	...	0.0821
SOUTHERN MISSOURI BANCORP, INC	2019	...	0.1092
UNITED BANCSHARES INC/OH	2016	...	0.0887
UNITED BANCSHARES INC/OH	2017	...	0.0799
UNITED BANCSHARES INC/OH	2018	...	0.0777
UNITED BANCSHARES INC/OH	2019	...	0.0830
STARRETT L S CO	2016	...	0.0038
STARRETT L S CO	2017	...	0.0038
STARRETT L S CO	2018	...	0.0038
STARRETT L S CO	2019	...	0.0028
ROCKWELL AUTOMATION, INC	2016	...	0.0021
ROCKWELL AUTOMATION, INC	2017	...	0.0020
ROCKWELL AUTOMATION, INC	2018	...	0.0021
ROCKWELL AUTOMATION, INC	2019	...	0.0030
...	...	...	...

time. For example, we can observe that Title 12 Part 1030 had the tendency to become more important for the Southern Missouri Bancorp over time, either because the company adjusted its business model (according to its self-disclosed description) in the direction of the act's content or the corresponding act was changed to regulate the corresponding company more stringently.

For some combinations of companies and Title-Parts, there is no calculation of regulatory exposure possible – in this case, either the Title-Part was not part of the CFR or the respective business description was not extractable (this is especially the case of older documents before the year 2000). However, this non-availability of some values means no loss of generality.

4.2 Results of Application to CFR

In this section, we investigate whether our framework reasonably gauges firm-specific regulatory exposure across different regulations and in the cross-section of companies. We evaluate whether our framework leads to economically plausible scores for regulatory exposure. Therefore, we rely on firms' industry classification using the North American Industry Classification System (NAICS), which reveals firms' business activities at a high level and which was also used by previous research [e.g., 1]. In the Subsection "Regulatory Exposure for Different NAICS Sectors", we analyze whether the average regulatory exposure score across all firms in a NAICS sector meaningfully relates to a given regulatory text. For instance, a firm with a NAICS code of 522120 ("Savings Institutions") should not have high exposure to, e.g., regulations around "Food and Drugs" (Title 21) but instead a higher exposure to regulations in the field "Banks and Finance". In the Subsection "Accuracy of Measuring Regulatory Exposure Across NAICS Sectors", we compute for a specific legal act the fraction of companies in a specific NAICS class that we expect a priori to be in the group of companies with the highest exposure to this act and we check whether this fraction is reasonably high.

Regulatory Exposure for Different NAICS Sectors. First, we scrutinize whether our framework is able to cluster firms operating in different industries according to their NAICS codes for a specific regulation. That is, we determine whether firms that operate in industries that we expect ex ante to have high exposure to the regulation under consideration actually have a high exposure using our measurement framework as introduced in Sect. 3.1. To do so, we choose a set of representative regulations and manually assess which firms are more (less) likely to be affected by the regulation. This step enables us to evaluate whether the computed regulatory exposure scores for firms are reasonably informative. We look here at broad industry definitions, at the 2-digits NAICS level, while the next subsection goes a step further and analyzes within-industry differences to have a more fine-grained representation of companies' activities.

As a first example, we consider again CFR Title 12 Part 1030 relating to the Truth in Savings Act passed in 1991 and part of a larger set of legal acts that are concerned with deposit insurance in the U.S. We analyze which firms and their corresponding industries are affected most in 2019. More specifically, we apply our framework to compute firm-level regulatory exposure using the Truth in Savings Act version as of end 2019 and companies' business description as disclosed in their respective 10-K filing for the fiscal year 2019. Figure 4 shows all firms' levels of regulatory exposure to this act. We group firms by their NAICS code and observe which industries exhibit higher or lower regulatory exposure. We represent firms within an industry via boxplots to depict information on the distribution of firms' regulatory exposure.

Our results in Fig. 4 indicate that firms in the "Finance and Insurance" industry reveal the highest median regulatory exposure to the Truth in Savings Act – which is in line with what we expected a priori from firms in this sector. Particularly, depository institutions within the finance and insurance institutions are mostly affected by regulation addressing deposit insurance. Moreover, companies in the area of "Education Services" reveal a high median regulatory exposure and the highest 75%-percentile value across all sectors. Looking into the business descriptions of these companies, we observe indeed relevant references to the topics related to "savings" because, in the U.S., education is tightly connected to the question of financing, e.g., credit grants and paying interest for credits. As expected, all other firms reveal lower average regulatory exposure. In other words, our framework is able to identify the relevance of legal acts for specific firms based on their self-disclosed information in their business descriptions. Our proposed framework indicates a higher exposure that can be interpreted by the company to take a closer look on the regulation to clarify the need to comply with it.

To further underline the applicability of our approach, we consider Title 34 Part 200 "Improving the Academic Achievement of the Disadvantaged" (Fig. 5) and Title 40 Part

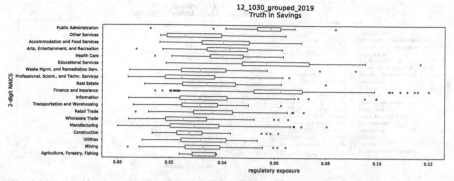

Fig. 4. Boxplot of firms' regulatory exposures grouped by 2-digit NAICS codes (Title 12, Part 1030, Truth in Savings Act, 2019). (Boxplot of firms' regulatory exposure to the Truth in Savings Act refers to the year 2019. Firms business descriptions are taken from fiscal year 2019 and the legal text is taken from a snapshot of the CFR at the end of 2019.)

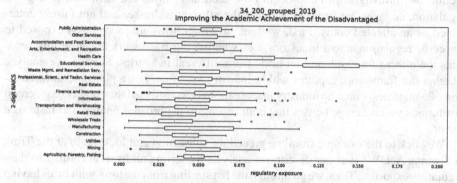

Fig. 5. Firms' regulatory exposure to Title 34 Part 200 in the year 2019 grouped by 2-digit NAICS codes ("Improving the Academic Achievement of the Disadvantaged").

177 "Issuance of Food Additive Regulations" (Fig. 6), i.e., two further examples of different industries. In Fig. 5, we see that the companies in the Educational Services sector reveal a distinctively higher regulatory exposure, e.g., their 25%-percentile is higher than the 75%-percentile of all over industries. This is in line with the expectations of an act regarding the improvement of academic achievements of particular disadvantaged groups. Regarding Title 40 Part 177, Fig. 6 shows that companies in the industry Health Care have the highest median exposure. This is a plausible finding since the use of food additives usually has to take into account health considerations for consumers. Here, the manufacturing industry exhibits the highest 75%-percentile value. This industry subsumes NAICS codes starting with 31 until 33 and while it includes companies with food activities, it also includes cement manufacturing or iron and steel, which are unaffected by a regulation on food additives. Therefore, the Subsection "Accuracy of Measuring Regulatory Exposure Across NAICS Sectors" will deliver results that are more detailed on this act by taking variation within these broad industry definitions into account.

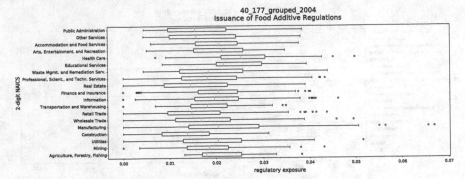

Fig. 6. Firms' regulatory exposure to Title 40 Part 177 in the year 2004 grouped by 2-digit NAICS codes ("Issuance of Food Additive Regulations").

Accuracy of Measuring Regulatory Exposure Across NAICS Sectors. In this sub-section, we investigate in more detail how accurately firms are attributed to a given regulation, i.e., whether firms are actually the relevant addressee and not falsely deter-mined as an affected entity. First, we look at which firms are more (less) exposed to a specific regulation across industries, i.e., whether our framework meaningfully sepa-rates the effect of a regulation on firms from different industries. Second, we analyze whether our framework captures within-industry variation, i.e., a plausible differentia-tion of companies within an industry that are more (less) affected than others (e.g., credit institutions vs. brokerage houses that both belong to the broader finance and insurance sector).

We stick to the example from the preceding subsection and look again at the Truth in Savings Act. We start our descriptive analysis by sorting all firms according to their regulatory exposure. Then, we go through the list starting from the top – with firms having the highest regulatory exposure based on our framework – and count how many firms have a relevant NAICS code, i.e., in our example again the finance and insurance sector. Similarly, when looking at the bottom of firms in terms of their regulatory exposure, we compute the fraction of firms that do not operate in the finance and insurance sector. Such top- and bottom-ranked validations are standard approaches and regularly used in the academic literature [e.g., 10]. For instance, among the top 10 firms, we find 8 firms that reveal a fitting NAICS code. Among the top 100 firms, 88 firms are associated with a relevant NAICS code. In general, the higher the fraction of firms that exhibit a matching NAICS code, the more accurately our framework works in assigning legal texts to relevant companies.

Figure 7 shows a graphical presentation of this analysis. The dotted (solid) line shows the fraction of firms (not) in the finance and insurance sector among the top (bottom) x firms in terms of the magnitude of their regulatory exposure score. The x-axis shows the number of firms in the top and bottom set of firms with the highest and lowest exposure scores, respectively. In the considered year 2019, among 3,065 firms in the data set, there are 535 firms that belong to the finance and insurance sector. Among the bottom 100 firms, 100 firms have a NAICS code that does not fit to the regulation. Even among the bottom 1,000 firms, 978 firms have a NAICS code that does not fit. Our overall result reveals that around 98% of the firms at the bottom 1,000 firms and around 92% of the top 200 firm are correctly classified in this example. This means that firms are sorted in a meaningful way and that our approach separates plausibly between high and low exposure firms.

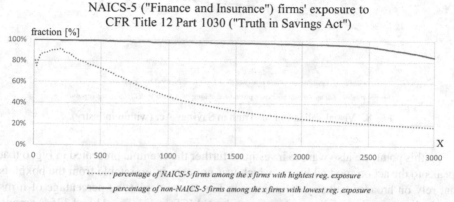

Fig. 7. Visual validation for the Truth in Savings Act (across industries).

Next, we check whether our framework is also able to differentiate between firms in a given industry that are more concerned by a regulation than other firms in the same industry. For example, the Truth in Savings Act should be more important for depository institutions compared to other financial institutions, e.g., investment banks or stock exchanges. Thus, we expect that depository institutions reveal higher regulatory exposure and are ranked higher compared to other financial institutions. Looking at the firms ranked by their regulatory exposure score, depository institutions should be more present in the top ranks, while other financial institutions should be found in relatively lower ranks. We identify depository institutions by their respective NAICS code, i.e., starting with 5221, and declare all other firms in the finance and insurance sector as non-depository institutions. Figure 8 shows the number of depository institutions (dotted line) compared to other finance and insurance institutions (solid line) among all finance and insurance institutions of the x top-ranked firms. For example, among the 10 (20) top-ranked companies, we find 8 (15) financial and insurance companies. All these 8 (15) companies are depository institutions. Among the 100 (1000) top-ranked companies, we find 88 (464) financial and insurance institutions. Thereof, 75 (324) companies are depository institutions (85.2%, 69,8%). Note, in the remaining set of financial and insurance companies, there are credit institutions included that might also have a relatively high exposure to the Truth in Savings Act and, thus, our results only represent a lower bound of the framework's accuracy. Overall, the figure implies that our framework is indeed able to rank those firms higher that have a closer relation to the topics of the regulation. Other finance and insurance institutions reveal a lower regulatory exposure on average. Thus, the framework is able to differentiate both between industries and on a within-industry level.

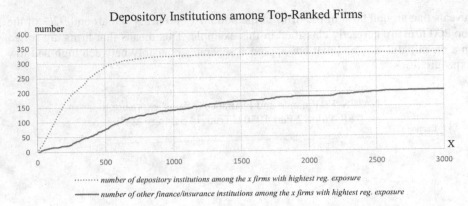

Fig. 8. Visual validation for Truth in Savings Act (within industry).

At this point, we also want to investigate further the example presented in Fig. 6 that speaks to the act on food additives, which was not easy interpretable from the boxplots that rely on broader industry definitions. In Fig. 9, we depict the percentage of firms that deal with food according to more granular NAICS codes (i.e., 31 and 3254) among the x top-ranked companies according to their regulatory exposure to CFR Title 40 Part 177 (dotted line). Moreover, the solid line depicts the percentage of non-food-related companies of the bottom-ranked companies. We can observe that the framework again attributes high regulatory exposure to those firms that deal with the act-related aspects. Among the 30 top-ranked companies, 24 companies are linked to NAICS 31 or 3254 (i.e., 80%).

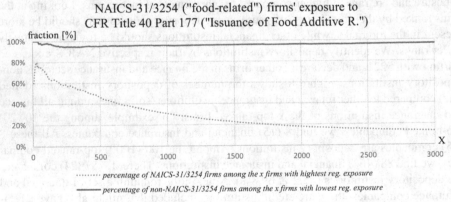

Fig. 9. Visual validation for the Issuance of Food Additive Regulation (across industries).

Next, we examine those companies that are top-ranked but not linked to NAICS codes 31 or 3254, i.e., the NAICS codes that deal with food. Interestingly, many of these companies are also concerned with the regulation although they have other NAICS codes. For example, we find companies of NAICS code 221310 (water supply and irrigation systems), companies that handle or pack food, or pharmaceutical companies, e.g., producing drugs that are consumed by patients. Including these companies increases the rate of correctly ranked companies considerably. According to Fig. 9, 69 of the 100 top-ranked companies are related to NAICS codes 31 or 3254. We analyze the top 100 companies manually and correct for companies subject to the act although not connected to NAICS codes 31 or 3254 and find that for 84 of the 100 top-ranked companies the act is of importance.

We conclude from these evaluation analyses that our framework is able to detect relevant characteristics of firms' business activities, i.e., products, and services, and reasonably links business descriptions to the textual content contained in regulations. While approaches to measure regulatory exposure at the industry level are limited to measure greater groups of firms by the same yardstick and do not take into account that firms often operate dynamically in multiple industry sectors, our framework allows to evaluate firms' regulatory exposure on a more fine-grained and firm-specific level.

5 Conclusion

We propose a novel framework for measuring regulatory exposure at the firm level relying on firms' self-disclosed business descriptions. While previous research has already proposed approaches for measuring regulatory exposure, there is no satisfying approach for measuring regulatory exposure at the firm level so far. Therefore, this paper contributes to close this gap.

Our proposed framework to quantify a firm's exposure to new or existing regulation bears relevant practical implications. On the one hand, our approach works as an information retrieval system by which firms can identify legal acts that are likely to affect their business. Using our approach, firms' legal departments can, for example, prioritize legal acts and further inspect specific pre-selected acts instead of manually investigating all new legal acts. This saves time and effort, and ultimately reduces firms' costs and burden to deal with regulation. On the other hand, our approach allows regulators to oversee the set of firms that are affected most by a particular regulation. Regulatory bodies can, then, monitor for each regulation separately the affected entities and evaluate their respective regulatory burden. So far, the industry-based approaches to measure regulatory exposure were only able to identify the affected industries. However, such approaches would rank all respective firms of an industry on the same level and the regulator cannot see for which firms the respective regulation might be of more or less importance. Here, our approach delivers added value and allows for considering firm-specific characteristics with more fine-grained nuances.

There are limitations to our approach: First, our framework depends on how well firms describe their business activities along the 10-K filings in our sample. Without detailed descriptions of firms' business activities, our framework cannot deliver optimal results. Second, we rely on yearly snapshots of legal documents that do not cover all interim versions of the regulations during the year. Nevertheless, this is a limitation of the analyzed data, not of our approach itself because it is also well applicable for legal acts enacted during the year and is not dependent on yearly snapshots. Third, some (usually larger) regulatory initiatives lead to a bundle of small and medium amendments throughout different Title-Parts. Our approach is able to indicate relevant Title-Parts separately, but is not intended to interpret complex legal structures, like connections between the documents.

Future research should address the case of interconnected amendments which are dispersed over the legal corpus – but which belong together – to better analyze the interplay of different Title-Parts and their combined effect on firms. Moreover, we focus on Title-Parts and do not differentiate for more granular substructures of the legal body. Future research is invited to consider this substructure for an even more detailed view on regulatory exposure. Finally, we are aware of the fact that the noun vectors could be further preprocessed in various ways, e.g., the introduction of particular weighting schemes that give a higher weight to more important nouns. In addition, future research could explore calculating textual similarity using pre-trained word vectors that we only used for the detection of nouns and the computation of synonyms. We leave it for future research to optimize the preprocessing steps to further enhance the measurement of regulatory exposure.

Acknowledgments. We thank the "efl – the Data Science Institute" located in Frankfurt am Main, Germany, for funding our project.

References

1. Al-Ubaydli, O., McLaughlin, P.A.: RegData: a numerical database on industry-specific regulations for all United States industries and federal regulations, 1997–2012. Regul. Gov. **11**(1), 109–123 (2017)
2. Caruana, J.: Financial Regulation, Complexity and Innovation. Bank for International Settlement, Promontory Annual Lecture, London (2014)
3. CFR: Truth in Savings (Regulation DD) (2021). https://www.ecfr.gov/current/title-12/chapter-X/part-1030. Accessed 16 Nov 2021
4. Dawson, J.W., Seater, J.J.: Federal regulation and aggregate economic growth. J. Econ. Growth **18**(2), 137–177 (2013)
5. Hoberg, G., Phillips, G.: Product market synergies and competition in mergers and acquisitions: a text-based analysis. Rev. Financ. Stud. **23**(10), 3773–3811 (2010)
6. Hoberg, G., Phillips, G.: Text-based network industries and endogenous product differentiation. J. Polit. Econ. **124**(5), 1423–1465 (2016)
7. Kalmenowitz, J.: Regulatory Intensity and Firm-Specific Exposure. Working Paper Version: 2021/10/29 (2021)
8. Katz, D., Ruhl, J.B.: Measuring, monitoring and managing legal complexity. IOWA Law Rev. **191**, 191–244 (2015)
9. Kitching, J., Hart, M., Wilson, N.: Burden or benefit? Regulation as a dynamic influence on small business performance. Int. Small Bus. J. **33**(2), 130–147 (2015). https://doi.org/10.1177/0266242613493454
10. Li, K., Mai, F., Shen, R., Yan, X.: Measuring corporate culture using machine learning. The Rev. Financ. Stud. **11**, 685 (2020)

11. Simões, P., Marques, R.C.: Influence of regulation on the productivity of waste utilities. What can we learn with the Portuguese experience? Waste Manag. (New York, N.Y.) **32**(6), 1266–1275 (2012). https://doi.org/10.1016/j.wasman.2012.02.004

12. de Smet, D.: Exploring the influence of regulation on the innovation process. Int. J. Entrep. Innov. Manag. **16**(1/2), 73–97 (2012)

13. Splatt, C.S.: Complexity of regulation. Harv. Bus. Law Rev. Online **3**, 1–9 (2012)

Realising Fair Outcomes from Algorithm-Enabled Decision Systems: An Exploratory Case Study

Franziska Koefer[1]([✉])([iD]), Ivo Lemken[2]([✉]), and Jan Pauls[3]

[1] University of Twente, Enschede, The Netherlands
f.koefer@utwente.nl
[2] University of Leiden, Leiden, The Netherlands
i.lemken@umail.leidenuniv.nl
[3] University of Muenster, Muenster, Germany
j.paul17@uni-muenster.de

Abstract. Fairness is a crucial concept in the context of artificial intelligence ethics and policy. It is an incremental component in existing ethical principle frameworks, especially for algorithm-enabled decision systems. Yet, translating fairness principles into context specific practices can be undermined by multiple unintended organisational risks. This paper argues that there is a gap between the potential and actual realized value of AI. Therefore, this research attempts to answer how organisations can mitigate AI risks that relate to unfair decision outcomes. We take a holistic view by analyzing the challenges throughout a typical AI product life cycle while focusing on the critical question of how rather broadly defined fairness principles may be translated into day-to-day practical solutions at the organizational level. We report on an exploratory case study of a social impact microfinance organization that is using AI-enabled credit scoring to support the screening process to particularly financially marginalized entrepreneurs. This paper highlights the importance of considering the strategic role of the organisation when developing and evaluating fair algorithm- enabled decision systems. The proposed framework and results of this study can be used to inspire the right questions that suit the context an organisation is situated in when implementing fair AI.

Keywords: Algorithm-enabled decision-systems · Fair AI · Microfinance · Fairness Principles · AI Life Cycle

1 Introduction

After more than half a century of flourishing academic research in fair AI, the most recent public initiatives resulted in the development of principles, guidelines and codes that may ethically guide organisations in the implementation and use of AI [15]. Recent work points towards further convergence of the large

© The Author(s), under exclusive license to Springer Nature Switzerland AG 2023
J. van Hillegersberg et al. (Eds.): FinanceCom 2022, LNBIP 467, pp. 52–67, 2023.
https://doi.org/10.1007/978-3-031-31671-5_4

emerging 'pool of AI principles' fostering coherence and compatibility of existing principles. This development comes to the aid of organisational actors who are hampered by the apparent lack of a unified AI terminology as well as fairness definition in order to implement fair AI [16,42]. At the same time researchers have called for caution towards 'algorithmic formalism' since prescribed definitions and abstractions may ignore the social complexity of the real world [21,30,48]. Unwanted biases in algorithms remain a challenge [12,30,45,48] that spring from so called 'abstraction traps' as practitioners fail to take into account the social context in which algorithms operate [45]. As a result, the achievement of fair AI in day-to-day organisational practices becomes more complex. This finding is also reflected in a survey which reports that 79% of tech workers are in need of more practical resources and guidance to help them with ethical considerations [14,35,37].

Without practical guidance, industry professionals are challenged by the many possibilities of interpreting abstract fairness principles [7]. As a result, organisations risk to become exposed to phenomena such as 'ethics blue washing' and 'ethics shirking' [15]. To limit organisational risks that are associated with the implementation of fair AI, research points towards the importance of involving the firm as a strategic player [17]. Rather than re-defining fairness frameworks, industry professionals need to ask context specific questions which create organizational awareness of fairness related risks and how AI influences it [31]. The debate should thus, evolve from what ethics are needed to how ethics can be successfully applied and implemented in context specific environments [47]. In return, organisations may limit fairness related AI- risks while at the same time implement AI systems that create the added value they were set out to have.

This study applies a context specific exploratory case study of a non-profit microfinance institution situated in the Netherlands. While adoption rates of AI in the microfinance industry have been slow, AI is increasingly becoming an integral component of firms strategies to achieve operational efficiency, improve customer service, and gain insights for competitive advantage. It is imperative that organizations understand the implications of this adoption from an AI risk and fairness perspective for two main reasons. First, given that the microfinance industry operates in a socially driven environment by delivering services that are life altering for marginalized clients, it is necessary to implement practices that ensure fair outcomes. Second, as pointed out in a recent literature review little fair AI research focuses on the financial sector despite its relevance for financial organizations and society. Bias in the financial sector, such as gender and race, could result in punishment by courts and fines [50].

We follow an AI product life cycle and analyse the implementation challenges organisations may encounter with AI technology. As a result, we elaborate on important aspects that should be considered when designing and deploying AI practices and mechanisms in financial organizations. These aspects ensure that main development challenges are overcome successfully and fair outcomes can be achieved.

The aim of the paper is to contribute to current research discourse on fair AI in the social finance literature by not only applying a context specific case. We also attempt to raise the Fair AI debate to a different level. We take a holistic view that guides the entire AI life cycle from the initial steps to the final outcome and its operation. In addition, we contribute to literature on decision support systems in particular. Our approach is meant to review the implementation and use of these systems so practitioners may be inspired to ask questions that suit the context of their organisation before unwanted organisational risks occur.

First, we define the relevant concepts of artificial intelligence, AI enabled decision systems and AI fairness before putting it in the context of financial services in the microfinance industry. After describing our research method, we present our framework and case study findings. Finally we discuss the implications of our findings and conclude this paper.

2   Theoretical Background

2.1   Artificial Intelligence and AI - Enabled Decision Systems

Artificial Intelligence has rapidly been gaining momentum in different industries. The term refers to the intelligence of machines, as directly opposed to human intelligence that is a natural intelligence residing in the brain [43]. Decision-makers have been immensely enabled by big data feeding AI systems to interpret economic or environmental contexts [39]. In general, the combination of technology, human perception, and organisations as interpretive systems enable information processing capabilities as well as understanding of the business environment [40]. Hence, AI systems if used ideally have the potential to create economic and social values for organizations and society.

2.2   Fairness and AI

The field of fair AI is concerned with the design, development, and implementation of an AI system as it ensures biases are removed. One of the main principles of AI ethics is fairness, which requires that AI is built in a manner that promotes democratic values and principles such as freedom and equality [28]. Algorithmic biases that produce discriminatory outcomes for certain groups of people may not only re-produce societal inequality, but also cause reputation damage to the organisation [19,50].

Nevertheless, the act of defining well-intended fairness principles in organisations may not be enough. For instance, the notion of equal treatment means that equal individuals should be treated equally irrespective of their demographic affiliation [11,18]. As this notion addresses procedural discrimination it suggests that organisations should exclude sensitive attributes from algorithmic input for their decision systems. This practice of equal treatment in algorithms often leads to unequal impact across demographic groups when there are systematic differences in groups [10,20,41,46]. To better achieve equal impact in algorithmic decision making policy debates have since evolved using notions such as equal opportunity, demographic parity, equalized odds, and conditional statistical parity [8,11,17,18,25,46]. While researchers argue that these notions incentives decision makers to build better algorithmic models [17,25], the importance of organisational learning upon which the accuracy of the algorithm depends is often being ignored [17]. To ensure an outcome that is fair, the strategic role of the organisation needs to be accounted for, in particular the costs of learning. This includes building a fitting organisational infrastructure as well as an experimental organisational environment [17].

2.3 Artificial Intelligence and Fairness in the Context of Financial Services in the Microfinance Industry

Microfinance institutions are financial intermediaries that pursue a lending strategy that serve disadvantaged borrowers. These disadvantages translate in information asymmetries, lack of credit history and disproportionate transaction costs when accessing small loans to start up a new business venture. Mostly vulnerable members of society, such as unemployed persons, young and elderly people, migrants, women and minorities are affected by these disadvantages [9].

Advances in AI enabled decision systems are consistently transforming the landscape in the previously relationship-oriented microfinance industry. In particular, credit scoring systems have expanded rapidly and are argued to increase the availability of credit to opaque and marginalized entrepreneurs as they improve the accuracy of risk-based pricing of loans. Credit scoring refers to the calculation of a single metric that expresses the creditworthiness of an individual [13]. Most credit scoring systems make use of machine learning, a subcategory of artificial intelligence, in which the system creates the rules itself. The development team only prepares the data as well as the function in order to evaluate the accuracy and precision of the model [24].

Research has shown that the inclusion of increasingly comprehensive databases as well as new methods of analysis help financial product developers (FinTechs) to deploy complex algorithms to predict the likelihood of repayment and profitability [29]. Nevertheless, integrating algorithmic systems in decision-making processes and existing business structures is raising concerns. Research particularly investigates the social welfare effects of permitting FinTech firms to operate in credit markets [29].

2.4 Existing Frameworks for Ethical Principles

In this section, two prominent ethical frameworks are being discussed. One framework was published by UNESCO. It was chosen, amongst others[1] because

---

[1] Other examples, such as the High-Level Expert Group on AI set up by the European Commission have a similar definition of the principle of fairness [26,27].

of its focus on fairness, upon which principles recommendations are built. Subsequently the AI-Blindspot framework by the MIT is discussed. The AI-Blindspot framework is being discussed due to its relevant life cycle model. It offers general guidelines to avoid unintended outcomes of the use of AI. The framework provided the key inspiration for the fairness-centered life cycle proposed in this paper.

The UNESCO Recommendation on the Ethics of Artificial Intelligence [6] has a dedicated section for fairness and non-discrimination in which three recommendations are written out: 1) AI needs to be accessible to everyone that wants to use it. This not only means finding a way for giving people access to the system, but also respecting specific needs based on "different age groups, cultural systems, different language groups, persons with disabilities, girls and women, and disadvantages, marginalized and vulnerable people or people in vulnerable situations" [6]. 2) Creators of AI systems need to make "reasonable efforts to minimize and avoid reinforcing or perpetuating discriminatory or biased applications". Additionally, there needs to be an easy and effective way to go into remedy against discrimination and biased algorithmic determination. [6] 3) Knowledge divides between countries and local communities have to be addressed in accordance with legal and regional frameworks, so that every person is treated equitably.

AI-Blindspot [36] is a tool developed by the MIT Media Lab, which provides a process for finding unintended outcomes of AI systems with a focus on machine learning as the most common technology in this field. It is stated that the consequences of such blind spots are difficult to foresee, but in nearly all cases marginalized communities are affected. To avoid blind spots a series of steps are proposed for the development and use of AI systems. The process is subdivided into 4 phases: Planning, building, deploying and monitoring. In the planning phase, the creator of the AI system needs to think about the purpose of the system, how representative the data is, if and how it can be abused and how privacy can be secured. In the building phase, the optimization criterion has to be set. This is very important for an AI system as the system tries to improve every indicator that is part of the optimization criterion and ignores all others. In the same step the explainability of the AI system has to be clarified. In the deploying phase, the creators have to set up a system to monitor the AI and react to any changes that may come over time, as well as offering individuals the right to contest [49]. The last phase is about monitoring the AI and frequently discussing with experts to ensure the AI system still fulfilling the same purpose it started with [36].

3   Method

A case study is a suitable research method for exploring complex new phenomena holistically and with a focus on "how" questions. Our exploratory case study uses documents and open publications retrieved from a non-profit microfinance institution. In addition, a pilot interview with two data analysts was used to identify personal experiences in the use of AI-supported credit scoring systems in the screening processes of credit applications. We have used semi-structured questionnaires during the interview to encourage a free flowing discussion [38], and encouraged the participants to provide examples of business situations where they observed challenges. Since the objective of microfinance is the delivery of services that can be life altering for marginalized clients, the chosen industry has special reasons to maintain consistent standards of eligibility to ensure fairness.

4 Framework Development

Fairness has many different levels and is often connected to, and sometimes seen as a synonym of, non-discrimination. However, Malgieri [34] shows that even within the limited context of GDPR [2] the principle of fairness is far more complex. It is being translated in different contexts as correctness, loyalty and equitability.

With this complexity in mind, it would be easy to think that fairness by design is impossible to reach, but any reasonable effort to get closer to it, should, in the authors opinion, be taken. Following the *UNESCO Recommendation on the Ethics of Artificial Intelligence* [6] we promote an inclusive approach that tries to minimize unfair and discriminatory outcomes and ensures effective remedy against unintended effects. Moreover, the large variety of available tools and frameworks to manage AI risks are often employed in isolation. A structured process that identifies when ethical failures (may) occur is necessary. This is why we take a holistic view by applying a life cycle framework.

4.1 The Life Cycle of AI Systems

Throughout the life cycle of an AI system, we identify the following five stages: problem statement, development, deployment, review & monitoring, and discontinuation (Table 1). These stages lean on the four stages of MIT Media Lab's AI Blindspot tool (planning, building, deploying and monitoring) [36], but is modified to use a more inclusive definition of AI and focus on fairness specifically. Furthermore, it is usable not only by actors that develop AI systems themselves, but also by those who acquire (existing) technologies from external suppliers.[2]

The Problem Statement Stage often starts naturally when organisations encounter a problem. In this stage it is important to create a clear definition of the problem. The definition is elemental to the choice of technology. It is important to identify individuals and groups that are at risk of suffering real

---

[2] This framework was furthermore based on common approaches on fairness extracted from literature reviews [16,37,48], and toolkits [1,3–5,44] that focus on ethical AI.

damage from negative outcomes when using the intended system. The questions should be raised whether there are known risks of unfairness in the chosen technology, explicate the fairness trade-offs and how risks can be mitigated or compensated for. Once the potential pitfalls are identified, the organisation can explicitly answer whether a technology delivers expected benefits and whether these outweigh the expected costs for all stakeholders.

Table 1. The five stages of the life cycle of a fair AI system.

Stage	Description
Problem statement	- Definition of the problem
	- Technology selection
	- Unfairness risk identification
	- Definition of steps to minimize risk of unfairness and ensure effective remedy
	- Continuation decision based on the positive and negative effects identified above
Development	- Implementation of the selected technology
	- Organizational process evaluation
	- Development of strategies for the "right to contest" and remedy
	- Equal opportunity strategy development
	- Explainability assessment
	- Unfairness risk and impact assessment
Deployment	- Evaluation of changes in the context of the system
	- Deployment of the system
	- Implementation of equal opportunity strategy
	- Implementation of right to contest and remedy strategy
Review & Monitoring	- Introduction of a formal oversight body
	- Regular stakeholder consultation
	- Continuous unfairness risk assessment
	- Continuous improvement identification
	- Definition of reasons for discontinuation
Discontinuation	- Suspension of the deployed system
	- Identification of persisting risks
	- Long-term remedy implementation

The Development Stage goes above programming of the chosen solution. We argue that it should incorporate the evaluation of current organizational processes and the development of new ones. This not only ensures a clearly identified path for any stakeholder to contest the automated decisions advice produced by the AI system but also remedy in case negative outcomes do lead to actual damage among individuals or groups of stakeholders. Furthermore, the explainability of the system should be assessed. If on any level the system is not explainable, the right to contest and implementation of remedies for unintended negative outcomes needs be clear within an organizational structure. Appropriate organisational processes to ensure above should be seen as the basis for an extensive unfairness impact assessment. In the ideal situation, these assessments can be done in public, but in cases where this is not possible, an independent audit could be considered depending on the level of impact that can be expected.

The Deployment Stage consists not only of the actual deployment of the system, but also the steps that should be taken before and alongside this process. An important step before deploying a system is to evaluate whether the context has changed in ways that impact its performance or the fairness of the outcome. Such changes can be small and context-specific, but also on a world-wide scale, like in the case of a pandemic. Next, the deployment should not begin without the implementation of strategies for equal opportunity, the right to contest and remedies. To support equal opportunity, it may be necessary to actively reach out to the most marginalized people so that they may benefit from your system.

The Review and Monitoring Stage consists of regularly organized reviews and continuous monitoring of all relevant changes in the context of the system. This stage requests a formal oversight body with sufficient authority.[3] This body should organize regular consultations with all stakeholders given that fairness related problems may escalate over time and go unnoticed. Fairness risk assessments can focus on incrementally changing external and internal organisational processes. In addition, potential improvements of the system itself can be identified. Finally, thresholds should be defined that may result in the discontinuation of the AI- decision system. For example, the AI-system should be discontinued when the risk of unfairness becomes so high, that effective remedy can no longer be guaranteed.

The Discontinuation Stage can be instantiated by "natural" processes, such as replacement by another system, but also by active interference by the oversight body, on the basis of unintended negative or unfair impact. It is always important to make an assessment of the risks that persist after discontinuation. These could be unfair situations that might escalate in the future, but also risks that come from re-usage of parts of the system. For these and other previously unnoticed unfair outcomes, a long-term remedy should be put into place in such a way that the negatively affected stakeholders have access to it.

---

[3] The oversight body is meant to prevent the opaqueness of AI systems and should provide regulation to prevent the common traps mentioned in [41]. The oversight body can be placed independently within the organization without interests that conflict with its role.

4.2 Framework Implementation

Since our framework uses an inclusive approach, it is recommended to combine it with toolkits and frameworks that are more specific to the situation and technology in use.[4] It is important to keep in mind that due to the variety of definitions of fairness, achieving fairness on one level, does not guarantee fairness on all levels. There are various examples of literature review studies that can be used to find guidance in the field of AI ethics [16,37,48] and toolkits [1,3–5,36,44] meant to tackle common ethical problems in AI. For any framework (including this one) to be effective, it should be adapted in such a way that it fits into the organizational environment [33].

5 Case Study

This section will give a short overview of the organization case study. The information has been collected from internal documentation at Qredits as well as publicly available reports, such as "Qredits: A Data-driven High-Tech Approach to European Microfinance. A Ten-Year perspective" [23].

5.1 Qredits - A Data-Driven Microfinance Institution with a Social Mission

Launched in January 2009, Qredits is a non-profit microfinance institution with a vision to build a strong and independent entrepreneurship culture in the Netherlands. Qredits achieves this by providing appropriate loan products, mentoring as well as educational tools for micro-entrepreneurs who wish to successfully start or invest in their business. The average loan size is 20.000 with which it supports small enterprises in the Netherlands. The organisation understands the lack of small loan sizes (between 5000–50.000 Euro) in the Dutch market as a failure of the market and has since then focused on fair financing of financially excluded start-up entrepreneurs in this market. For instance, a recent social impact report shows that 12,1% of entrepreneurs they serve have migration background, 16% unemployed, 19% above the age 50 have received support to help them create a career in the Netherlands.

Qredits business case could have not been possible without the use of technology. Foremost due to cost and time-efficiency reasons, one of the most important technologies introduced are those that improve insights that can be gathered about the entrepreneur and/or his/her business. The non- profit feeds its algorithm from different data sources, such as historical data points, Chamber of Commerce and PSD2 enabled bank data (since 2020). This enables risk assessing loan advisors to have a more informed input before making decisions on the creditworthiness of a loan request.

---

[4] Such as the seven dimensions framework for machine learning systems provided by [22] and further analyzed by [32].

The institution introduced its own machine-based risk score in 2017 to predict early signs of risk during the assessment of new applications. The machine-based risk score is useful in analysing collected data and increasing efficiencies of the decision-making process by combining over 1,200 data variables that may indicate potential risks. Scores range from 0 to 10 and are provided as complementary information source for the loan officer. While applicants will never be rejected based on the initial risk score, a score between 0 and 6 may indicate a higher probability of loan risks. A benchmark of 7 or higher may trigger access to the Fast Track screening process. This means that client visits are not necessary speeding up the screening process. Nevertheless, it is up to the discretion of the loan officer to deviate from the initial score recommendation and request a follow up meeting [23].

5.2   Preliminary Findings

This section elaborates on the preliminary findings in each stage of the life cycle of AI systems on fair decisions.

The Problem Statement Stage: The preliminary investigation into the problem statement stage resulted in some practical questions:

First, the interviewees have pointed out that while microfinance as an industry itself is not known for highly autonomous processes, AI supported workflows are becoming more common. The industry is undergoing changes throughout the last decade thanks to the growing competition in the financial technology (FinTech) industry. Due to new technologies, operation costs of many financial service providers have decreased and the time to process an application has become shorter. Thus, in 2017 Qredits implemented the credit score to strategically support the application process.

Second, the choice of technology was guided by a clear definition of how the technology should be used and what it should aim to achieve: Decisions on the creditworthiness of an applicant should not solely be based on the credit score output as the company still envisions a close relationship with its customers throughout the screening and monitoring phase. However, the relationship between technology and loan professional is envisioned in such a way that it will speed up the application process without disadvantaging marginalized client groups. When asking whether the expected benefits outweighed the expected costs when implementing the tool, the interviewees were aware of the likelihood that marginalized groups may not benefit from the implementation of the tool directly.

Third, fairness to marginalized groups may be achieved due to loan professionals freeing up time for more risky borrowers (i.e. for additional in-person meetings etc.) while less risky clients can simply be processed more quickly thanks to the risk score indication.

Thus the company may raise the following questions to mitigate risk of implementing unfair AI:

- Does the development of the technology undermine the company's mission?
- To what extent is the tool solving issues for our stakeholders, including, data analysts, marginalized borrowers, loan advisors?

The Development Stage: The interviewees recognized that there was no clearly identified path for stakeholders to contest the results of the credit score. Nevertheless, given the size of the institution it seemed as though an unofficial process was in place that gave loan professionals and risk managers the right to contest the results. An example was given during the interview. At the time that the score was implemented, there was a lot of confusion of either too high or too low scores that did not add up with the opinion of the professionals. Hence, a communication process between data analysts, loan professionals and risk managers established via email or in person to evaluate, explain and adjust the outcome of the score.

In addition, it should be mentioned that Qredits is working with a product supplier who has been supporting the development of the statistical model. Throughout the interview they recognized the lack of checks in place that would ensure the quality of data, such as robustness and reliability.

Nevertheless, the company believes that since the model only using objective variables, rather than demographic data, such as gender and country of origin, the model should not lead to a negative/unfair outcome. Thus it seems, non-discrimination is taken into account.

Thus the company may raise the following questions to mitigate risk of implementing unfair AI:

- Does the supplier of the technology offer quantitative data to support the statement that the technology offers a fair outcome?
- Whilst stakeholders should have the right to contest the results, have there been independent checks in place that have the ability to check unintended negative outcomes?

The Deployment Stage: External shocks have had quite an impact on the performance of the score in terms of fairness as the statistical model did not consider the changed situation for shop owners and entrepreneurs affected by the corona crisis. Hence, whilst the data analysts are aware that the statistical model needs recalibration, the score is still being relied on and in used. Changes to the statistical model are planned to be made in 2022.

The company encountered some issues in the deployment and the monitoring stage which are mostly related to missing methods to help them identify numerically if the score output will lead to fair outcomes. On one side the feedback from professional loan officers regarding the score output supports the process, but is mostly subjective. On the other side it has been an issue for Qredits to measure the impact of the AI-enabled score output. This is due to fact that Type 1 and Type 2 errors can only be measured over several years. For example, the company can check whether the score output of 8 (Low Risk) was true once the customer has repaid, or his/her company achieved his/her targets. Besides relying on subjective feedback of the loan professionals, Qredits will be able to take more data into account in the coming year that will allow them to check reliably for biases, discrimination or unfair treatment.

Thus the company may raise the following questions to mitigate risk of implementing unfair AI:

- Have we considered changing circumstances, such as external shocks into our statistical model and has it created unfair outcomes?
- Are there industry specific difficulties in testing and measuring whether the score outcome is robust, correct and fair?

The Review and Monitoring Stage: According to the interviewees there is no oversight body in place that would review AI Fairness as risk within a separate agenda point, in addition to the other risks that needs to be assessed, i.e. default risks, operational risks, equity risks etc. Moreover, there seems to be a purpose behind the lack of transparency of the algorithm for most stakeholders. Whilst data analysts have access to the information of what drives a score up and down, it has been deliberately decided to keep this information a black box to organizational stakeholders. Reasons are not entirely clear. Moreover, the competitive market at the time when the score was introduced also led to the decision to not bother stakeholders with the details of the algorithms. Nevertheless, the interviewees noted that since the score only uses objective variables there should be no reason to keep the information in a black box and the issue has already been discussed on the executive level.

Thus the company may raise the following questions to mitigate risk of implementing unfair AI:

- Are there context specific reasons why transparency as well as explainability of our AI tool should be minimized?
- If so, how can we find workarounds of this deficit that still mitigates risks of unfair AI due to a lack of transparency and explainability of the statistical model?

The Discontinuation Stage: The risk score was implemented in 2017 only, hence the product has not reached its discontinuation stage yet in the life cycle. Nevertheless, the investigation has raised many questions that require further research by the company to clarify and identify what kind of tools and practices they could deploy to ensure that the risk of unfair outcomes is mitigated.

6 Discussion and Conclusion

The framework introduced in this paper is intended to provide questions that can guide thinking processes inside organizations when aiming to implement fair AI systems. The case study, which focuses on a non-profit microfinance institution, provides good insights into the existing practices as well as challenges when implementing fairness principles in practice. While some principles, such as the right to contest, were already implemented, albeit in an informal way, others were not. However, the value of these principles was acknowledged by the interviewees and further recommendations could be made to the company based on the framework introduced in this paper. There are three major findings the authors wish to raise.

Firstly, within our framework we identified a large risk of unfair AI when problems go unnoticed (i.e. in a black box system) and may escalate over time. Only through existing feedback loops which momentarily exists between the loan professionals and data analysts in our case study, the credit score output is continuously being questioned and adjusted. Secondly, the findings indicate the importance of understanding the strategic role of the company in influencing the use of the algorithm-enabled decision system [17]. For example, the company in our case study aims to keep loan professionals in the assessment loop for relationship purposes with the customer. This approach aligns with the company's values and vision. Hence, it may further impede the establishment of a method that ensures fair algorithm-enabled decision outcomes. Thirdly and importantly, it becomes apparent that the company perceives the notion of fairness as equal treatment of applications. This becomes evident in their believe that the score output can not be discriminatory as it only uses objective variables as model input. However, as pointed out by previous research, further investigations should ensure that AI-enabled decision systems take into account existing systematic inequality between groups, which means treating customers up to the same standards may lead to unfair outcomes, and re-produce existing inequalities [10, 20, 41, 46].

The preliminary findings show no concrete obstacles to implement the framework in practice, at least in the case of our case study. However, the results have to be seen with caution. As our collected data is only provided by one company active in the space, it is not very representative. Further research may apply the framework to a larger group of organizations and therefore give a more representative view. Additionally, further research can apply our framework do different domains to get a wider overview for the practical application. Lastly, the framework proposed in our paper is technology-agnostic and does not imply the use of a specific AI technology. Therefore, it is very important to not solely rely on it, but instead combine it with more in-detail frameworks that correspond to a specific context to prevent technology-specific risks like biased data collection for machine learning systems. Furthermore, this approach is focused on fairness, but other elements of ethical AI should be taken into account.[5]

---

[5] There is no clear consensus on the priorities and subdivisions in the ethics of AI, but several overarching frameworks are mentioned in Sect. 2.4.

To conclude, the preliminary findings provide great insights into the application of the proposed framework for fairness in AI and AI enabled-systems. Its holistic approach will hopefully inspire further research to investigate how ethical principles can be implemented in context specific environments, such as microfinance in order to realise the value an AI technology has set out to achieve.

References

1. Ethics & algorithms toolkit. https://ethicstoolkit.ai/. Accessed 15 Jan 2022
2. Regulation (EU) 2016/679 of the European parliament and of the council of 27 April 2016 on the protection of natural persons with regard to the processing of personal data and on the free movement of such data, and repealing directive 95/46/EC (general data protection regulation) (text with EEA relevance). http://data.europa.eu/eli/reg/2016/679/2016-05-04
3. Algorithmic accountability policy toolkit. Technical report, AI Now Institute at New York University (2018)
4. Consequence scanning: An agile event for responsible innovators (2019). https://doteveryone.org.uk/project/consequence-scanning/. Accessed 15 Jan 2022
5. Examining the black box: Tools for assessing algorithmic systems. Technical report, Ada Lovelace Institute (2020)
6. Report of the social and human sciences commission (SHS). Technical report 41 C/73, UNESCO (2021)
7. Alshammari, M., Simpson, A.: Towards a principled approach for engineering privacy by design. In: Schweighofer, E., Leitold, H., Mitrakas, A., Rannenberg, K. (eds.) APF 2017. LNCS, vol. 10518, pp. 161–177. Springer, Cham (2017). https://doi.org/10.1007/978-3-319-67280-9_9
8. Barocas, S., Selbst, A.D.: Big data's disparate impact. Calif. Law Rev., 671–732 (2016)
9. Canales, R., Greenberg, J.: A matter of (relational) style: loan officer consistency and exchange continuity in microfinance. Manage. Sci. **62**(4), 1202–1224 (2016)
10. Chouldechova, A., Benavides-Prado, D., Fialko, O., Vaithianathan, R.: A case study of algorithm-assisted decision making in child maltreatment hotline screening decisions. In: Conference on Fairness, Accountability and Transparency, pp. 134–148. PMLR (2018)
11. Corbett-Davies, S., Goel, S.: The measure and mismeasure of fairness: a critical review of fair machine learning. arXiv preprint arXiv:1808.00023 (2018)
12. Edwards, L., Veale, M.: Slave to the algorithm: why a right to an explanation is probably not the remedy you are looking for. Duke L. Tech. Rev. **16**, 18 (2017)
13. Finlay, S.: Credit Scoring, Response Modeling, and Insurance Rating: A Practical Guide to Forecasting Consumer Behavior. Palgrave Macmillan (2012)
14. Floridi, L.: Establishing the rules for building trustworthy AI. Nat. Mach. Intell. **1**(6), 261–262 (2019)
15. Floridi, L.: Translating principles into practices of digital ethics: five risks of being unethical. In: Floridi, L. (ed.) Ethics, Governance, and Policies in Artificial Intelligence. PSS, vol. 144, pp. 81–90. Springer, Cham (2021). https://doi.org/10.1007/978-3-030-81907-1_6
16. Floridi, L., Cowls, J.: A unified framework of five principles for AI in society. In: Floridi, L. (ed.) Ethics, Governance, and Policies in Artificial Intelligence. PSS, vol. 144, pp. 5–17. Springer, Cham (2021). https://doi.org/10.1007/978-3-030-81907-1_2

17. Fu, R., Aseri, M., Singh, P., Srinivasan, K.: "un" fair machine learning algorithms. Manage. Sci. **68**, 4173–4195 (2022)
18. Fu, R., Huang, Y., Singh, P.V.: AI and algorithmic bias: source, detection, mitigation and implications. Detect. Mitigat. Implications (July 26, 2020) (2020)
19. Fu, R., Huang, Y., Singh, P.V.: Crowds, lending, machine, and bias. Inf. Syst. Res. **32**(1), 72–92 (2021)
20. Fuster, A., Goldsmith-Pinkham, P., Ramadorai, T., Walther, A.: Predictably unequal? The effects of machine learning on credit markets. J. Financ. **77**(1), 5–47 (2022)
21. Green, B., Viljoen, S.: Algorithmic realism: expanding the boundaries of algorithmic thought. In: Proceedings of the 2020 Conference on Fairness, Accountability, and Transparency, pp. 19–31 (2020)
22. Greene, D., Hoffmann, A.L., Stark, L.: Better, nicer, clearer, fairer: a critical assessment of the movement for ethical artificial intelligence and machine learning. In: Proceedings of the 52nd Hawaii International Conference on System Sciences (2019)
23. Groenevelt, E.: Qredits: a data-driven high-tech approach to European microfinance. a ten-year perspective (2019). https://cdn.qredits.nl/shared/files/documents/qredits-a-data-driven-high-touch-approach-to-european-microfinance.pdf
24. Gunnarsson, B.R., vanden Broucke, S., Baesens, B., Óskarsdóttir, M., Lemahieu, W.: Deep learning for credit scoring: do or don't? Eur. J. Oper. Res. **295**(1), 292–305 (2021). https://www.sciencedirect.com/science/article/pii/S037722172100196X
25. Hardt, M., Price, E., Srebro, N.: Equality of opportunity in supervised learning. Adv. Neural Inf. Process. Syst. **29**, 292–305 (2016)
26. High-Level Expert Group on Artificial Intelligence: Ethics guidelines for trustworthy AI (2019)
27. High-Level Expert Group on Artificial Intelligence: Assessment list for trustworthy AI (ALTAI) (2020)
28. Ienca, M.: Democratizing cognitive technology: a proactive approach. Ethics Inf. Technol. **21**(4), 267–280 (2019)
29. Johnson, K., Pasquale, F., Chapman, J.: Artificial intelligence, machine learning, and bias in finance: toward responsible innovation. Fordham L. Rev. **88**, 499 (2019)
30. Katell, M., et al.: Toward situated interventions for algorithmic equity: lessons from the field. In: Proceedings of the 2020 Conference on Fairness, Accountability, and Transparency, pp. 45–55 (2020)
31. Lee, M.S.A., Floridi, L., Denev, A.: Innovating with confidence: embedding AI governance and fairness in a financial services risk management framework. In: Floridi, L. (ed.) Ethics, Governance, and Policies in Artificial Intelligence. PSS, vol. 144, pp. 353–371. Springer, Cham (2021). https://doi.org/10.1007/978-3-030-81907-1_20
32. Lo Piano, S.: Ethical principles in machine learning and artificial intelligence: cases from the field and possible ways forward. Hum. Soc. Sci. Commun. **7**(1), 1–7 (2020)
33. Madaio, M.A., Stark, L., Wortman Vaughan, J., Wallach, H.: Co-designing checklists to understand organizational challenges and opportunities around fairness in AI. In: Proceedings of the 2020 CHI Conference on Human Factors in Computing Systems. ACM, New York (2020)
34. Malgieri, G.: The concept of fairness in the GDPR: a linguistic and contextual interpretation. In: Proceedings of the 2020 Conference on Fairness, Accountability,

and Transparency, FAT* 2020, pp. 154–166. Association for Computing Machinery, New York (2020)

35. Miller, C., Coldicott, R.: People, power and technology: the tech workers' view (2019). https://doteveryone.org.uk/report/workersview

36. MIT Media Lab: AI blindspot: a discovery process for preventing, detecting, and mitigating bias in AI systems (2019). https://aiblindspot.media.mit.edu/. Accessed 13 Jan 2022

37. Morley, J., Floridi, L., Kinsey, L., Elhalal, A.: From what to how: an initial review of publicly available AI ethics tools, methods and research to translate principles into practices. In: Floridi, L. (ed.) Ethics, Governance, and Policies in Artificial Intelligence. PSS, vol. 144, pp. 153–183. Springer, Cham (2021). https://doi.org/10.1007/978-3-030-81907-1_10

38. Moustakas, C.: Phenomenological Research Methods. Sage Publications (1994)

39. Namvar, M.: Using business intelligence to support the process of organizational sensemaking. Ph.D. thesis, Deakin University (2016)

40. Namvar, M., Intezari, A.: Wise data-driven decision-making. In: Dennehy, D., Griva, A., Pouloudi, N., Dwivedi, Y.K., Pappas, I., Mäntymäki, M. (eds.) I3E 2021. LNCS, vol. 12896, pp. 109–119. Springer, Cham (2021). https://doi.org/10.1007/978-3-030-85447-8_10

41. O'neil, C.: Weapons of math destruction: how big data increases inequality and threatens democracy. Crown (2016)

42. Peters, D., Calvo, R.: Beyond principles: a process for responsible tech (2019). https://medium.com/ethics-of-digital-experience/beyond-principles-a-process-for-responsible-tech-aefc921f7317

43. Poole, D., Mackworth, A., Goebel, R.: Computational Intelligence. Oxford University Press, Oxford (1998)

44. PricewaterhouseCoopers: PwC's responsible AI toolkit. https://www.pwc.com/gx/en/issues/data-and-analytics/artificial-intelligence/what-is-responsible-ai.html. Accessed 15 Jan 2022

45. Selbst, A.D., Boyd, D., Friedler, S.A., Venkatasubramanian, S., Vertesi, J.: Fairness and abstraction in sociotechnical systems. In: Proceedings of the Conference on Fairness, Accountability, and Transparency, pp. 59–68 (2019)

46. Skeem, J.L., Lowenkamp, C.T.: Risk, race, and recidivism: predictive bias and disparate impact. Criminology **54**(4), 680–712 (2016)

47. Taddeo, M., Floridi, L.: How AI can be a force for good – an ethical framework to harness the potential of AI while keeping humans in control. In: Floridi, L. (ed.) Ethics, Governance, and Policies in Artificial Intelligence. PSS, vol. 144, pp. 91–96. Springer, Cham (2021). https://doi.org/10.1007/978-3-030-81907-1_7

48. Tsamados, A., et al.: The ethics of algorithms: key problems and solutions. In: Floridi, L. (ed.) Ethics, Governance, and Policies in Artificial Intelligence. Philosophical Studies Series, vol. 144. Springer, Cham (2021). https://doi.org/10.1007/978-3-030-81907-1_8

49. Wachter, S., Mittelstadt, B., Russell, C.: Counterfactual explanations without opening the black box: automated decisions and the GDPR (2017)

50. Xivuri, K., Twinomurinzi, H.: A systematic review of fairness in artificial intelligence algorithms. In: Dennehy, D., Griva, A., Pouloudi, N., Dwivedi, Y.K., Pappas, I., Mäntymäki, M. (eds.) I3E 2021. LNCS, vol. 12896, pp. 271–284. Springer, Cham (2021). https://doi.org/10.1007/978-3-030-85447-8_24

The Effect of Changes in Interest Rate Regulation on the Financial Performance of Banks in Kenya

Jane Ngaruiya[1]([✉]), Pat Obi[2], and David Mathuva[1]

[1] Strathmore University Business School, Strathmore University, Nairobi, Kenya
{Jane.ngaruiya,dmathuva}@strathmore.edu
[2] Purdue University Northwest, Hammond, IN, USA
obi@pnw.edu

Abstract. The purpose of this study is to assess the effect of changes in interest rate regulation on the financial performance of banks in Kenya. Using a panel dataset of 78 banks in East Africa comprising 1,278 observations over the period 2004–2019, we employ difference-in-difference methodology on accounting and market value measures of financial performance. Two-step generalised method of moments, is used as the estimation technique to address the problem of endogeneity, commonly found in panel data. The results, which are robust for endogeneity and other checks reveal that introduction of interest rate caps in Kenya significantly increased the profitability of banks. This increase can likely be attributed to increase in non-interest income and reduction in operating expenses. On the contrary, the impact on publicly listed banks was insignificant. The study has the potential to inform policy makers in the East Africa region on the effects of interest rate regulation. High lending interest rates has seen some countries such as Kenya impose interest rate caps and subsequently repealed. Other countries such as Uganda were in the process of considering rate caps but have deferred the decision. The study is perhaps the first to examine the effect of changes in interest rate regulation on the financial performance of countries in the East African region. The authors also employ difference-in-difference methodology and two-step generalised method of moments estimation (GMM) in the study which is different from previous studies.

Keywords: Interest rate regulation · Bank performance · Tobin-Q · Difference-in-differences · Kenya · East Africa

1 Introduction

Interest rate is one of the important macroeconomic variables and is directly related to economic growth. Interest rate regulation in most countries resurfaced in the aftermath of the Global Financial Crisis (GFC) 2008–2009. The economic effects of imposing interest rate controls largely depend on how banks adjust supply and composition of credit in response to the policy. Consumers adjust their demand for credit when faced with the changes in supply by banks and magnitude of the difference between the market interest rate and the nominal value of the interest rate cap (Safavian and Zia 2018).

Despite the good intentions of interest rate regulations, international experience shows that in most cases interest rate controls have produced negative outcomes such as reduced bank competition, increased risk to financial stability, reduced transparency by banks and reduction in credit supply to high-risk borrowers hindering economic growth (Central Bank of Kenya [CBK] 2018). In the absence of effective competition, high interest rate spreads lead to above-normal profits provoking interest rate regulation. This was the case in Kenya. Despite interest rate controls being commonly used in the world, studies on the effect of imposition of interest rate controls on financial markets are relatively sparse (Alper et al. 2019).

This study aims to assess the impact of changes in interest rate regulation. This paper unlike previous studies, determines the causal impact of changes in interest rate regime in comparison with other East Africa countries. There is lack of empirical evidence on the impact of interest rate controls and this study contributes to literature. Overall, our results reveal that changes interest rate regulation is significant to bank financial performance. Our results therefore, are in favour of imposition of interest rate controls to regulate lending rates charged by commercial banks.

The remainder of the paper is structured as follows: In Sect. 2, interest rate regulation and banks performance in Kenya and in Sect. 3, literature review and hypotheses development. In Sect. 4, methodology and in Sect. 5, results and discussion. Section 6, conclusion and further research suggestions.

2 Interest Rate Regulation and Bank Performance in Kenya

In the 1990s, there was financial liberalisation in Kenya during which interest rates were determined by market forces. During this period, there was increased competition in the banking industry (Ngugi 2001). Globally, banks in Africa were found to be more profitable even though the continent continues to experience low levels of financial intermediation (Flamini et al. 2009). Oddly however, banks enjoyed double digit interest rate spreads for many years. Many consumers and policy makers complained that banks were charging usury interest rates on their loans while paying minuscule interest rates on customer deposits. In response, the Central Bank of Kenya (CBK) introduced interest rate capping in September 2016 (Matundura 2018).

The Central Bank of Kenya (Amendment) Bill 2001 popularly known as the Donde Bill was introduced in 2001 to reintroduce regulation of interest rates in Kenya. The Bill sought to peg interest rates to Treasury bill (TBs) rates as well as establish a Monetary Policy Committee (MPC) at CBK. However, the Bill was declared by the courts to be void because of its retrospective application. Amendment of Kenya Banking Act no. 9 in 2006 introduced in duplum law in Kenya. In duplum law protects the consumer as it provides that in respect to non-performing loans (NPL), unpaid interest should stop accruing once it equals the unpaid principal amount borrowed. In Kenya, interest rate caps were introduced in 2015 through a proposal made in parliament. The bill was finally assented by the President on the 24th of August 2016. The Bill sought to amend section 33A of the Banking Act by introducing a new section (section 33B) which provides for interest ceilings, giving a warning to the borrowers to be aware of the interest they receive on their deposits and repercussions to all financial institutions that carry out the function of lending on providing interest rates higher than those set by the law.

Section 33B (1) (b) of the Banking Amendment Bill also said that any Kenyan with a savings account in a bank will receive a predetermined interest rate on the deposit with the reference rate being the Central Bank rate (CBR) (Safavian and Zia 2018). This clause set the minimum interest rate that a bank would pay for a savings deposit at 70% of the base rate set by the Central Bank of Kenya. This is to mean that with a CBR of 10%, the minimum amount of interest payable for a savings account is 7% and the maximum interest charged on loans is 14% which is 400 basis points above the CBR. The legislation's main aim was to restrict banking institutions from setting extremely high interest rates on loans and exceptionally low interest rates on deposits. Specifically, the law prescribed that no banking institution that issued a loan would charge an interest rate that is more than 400 basis points above a base rate set by the Central Bank of Kenya. For the bank client who seeking a loan, it was possible to predict the maximum interest on a loan to be provided using the base rate as would be declared by the Central Bank (Aglionby 2016). Consequently, interest rate spreads fell sharply to single digits (Kavwele et al. 2018). Alper et al. (2019) posits that combination of floors on deposits with ceilings on lending rates is exceptionally rare. Furthermore, it was noted that no other country had imposed stringent caps like Kenya. The law did not apply on non-deposit taking microfinance institutions (MFIs), savings credit cooperatives (SACCOs), and mobile money banking or related financial transactions. In September 2018, under the Finance Bill Act 2018, the floor on the interest rate offered for time deposits was repealed. Section 33b of the Banking Act Caps was repealed on 7 November 2019. Central Bank continues to monitor interest rates charged by commercial banks.

A sound competition in the financial services sector is vital to the economy because it improves quality of financial products and degree of financial innovation. Bank competition also improves access to financial services for households and firms (Amidu 2020). Furthermore, in the long-run bank competition corrects the negative effects of high interest rates and wide interest rate spreads caused by bank profitability (Flamini et al. 2009).

The level of bank competition in Kenya is low leading to inefficiency in the market. This requires the intervention of the government to ensure financial intermediation. The domination by large and medium sized banks can be eliminated by merger of smaller banks (Mdoe et al. 2013). In addition, there exists monopolistic competition in Kenya which has a positive impact on the GDP (Ombongi and Long 2018).

Mdoe et al. (2019) posits that banks in Kenya position themselves by using technology to improve service delivery and diversify their products. This has increased bank competition but reduced profitability though in the short run. Furthermore, Atiti et al. (2020) noted that there is a negative relationship between bank competition and stability therefore, there is need for proactive policy measures by the regulator. Competition increases risk taking by banks. Excessive competition erodes market power and net margins driving commercial banks to take more risks.

3 Literature Review and Hypothesis Development

Financial intermediaries exist to reduce transaction costs and asymmetry of information between agents (borrowers and lenders). Intermediaries therefore aim to enhance these issues created by transaction and information agents. This is through facilitation of savings, pooling and diversification of risks, and allocation of resources (Leland and Pyle 1977). Banks role as financial intermediaries incur transaction costs since the receipts for deposits and loans are not synchronized. A price is charged for the intermediation services and set the interest rate levels for loans and deposits. The costs are defined by the difference between gross costs of borrowing (deposits) and the net return on lending (Ngugi 2001). In a market where there is perfect competition, the wedge between the lending rates and deposit is narrower while in imperfect competition, the wedge is wider reflecting inefficiencies in the market.

Financial intermediation exists where a third party whose purpose is to facilitate transfer of information or wealth between two other parties. Intermediation involves taking risk, and intermediaries' ability to lend is compromised when they suffer losses. Commercial banks can create money, for example by lending to businesses and home buyers, and accepting deposits backed by those loans. The amount of money created by financial intermediaries depends crucially on the health of the banking system and on the presence of profitable investment opportunities in the economy (Allen and Santomero 1998). In addition, Allen and Gale (2004) argue that financial institutions do exist for facilitation of efficient allocation of resources and risks. Any government intervention through monetary policies will have an impact on the normal functioning of the financial system in an economy. Monetary policies preventing financial crises will eventually create distortions in the market.

Most traditional theories of intermediation are based on asymmetry of information and transaction costs. Akerlof (1970) lodged the lemon principle. This is where one party in a transaction has more information than the other therefore at an advantage. This also makes it difficult to distinguish good quality from bad especially in the business world. In the insurance industry, those who are over 65 years or deemed to be riskier will end up paying more than those who are not. That is, the price levels increase to match the risk. In this principle, those who are aware they are riskier are willing to pay more. This leads to the aspect of adverse selection. This arises in commercial banks because banks gather information about their customers and use the same to charges them interest rates. Banks learn more about their customers than other banks would therefore have an advantage (Sharpe 1990). Financial intermediation theories are always based on some cost advantage for the intermediary. These are also known as delegation costs which are high at times therefore, costly to use an intermediary (Diamond 1984).

Allen and Santomero (1998) argue that current theories of intermediation are not a concern in a developed economy therefore the need to look at other functions of intermediation. These new functions include facilitators of risk transfer. Risk management has become a common phenomenon of intermediation though not clear why financial institutions should perform this important function. This is because financial intermediaries are in the business of trading financial assets that have a risk component. To enhance intermediation efficiency, competition among commercial banks is critical. In the long-run, competition in the banking industry improves the negative feature of intermediation efficiency that manifests in bank profitability which is mainly driven by high interest rates and wide interest rate spreads. Competition is important among commercial banks as it enhances access to credit, allocation of capital and innovation of financial products (Flamini et al. 2009).

The financial market intermediation theory explains the role of financial intermediaries as bridging the gap between the lenders and borrowers. If the financial market is perfect, the price charged would be at equilibrium while if an imperfect market, the price charged is higher or lower. This clarifies that the high interest rates charged by commercial banks are to some extent due to an imperfect financial market hence to mitigate this, the government uses monetary policy tools like interest rate regulation. On the other hand, current theorist advocate for free market as this leads to competition and increases efficiency in the financial market. Monetary policies such as ceilings on interest rates distort the market. The component of risk needs to be factored by financial intermediaries.

Matundura (2018) echoed that interest regulation in Kenya led to a decrease in the profitability of commercial banks. This was because with the introduction of caps in 2016, banks were not offering unsecured loans to high-risk individuals and organizations. This also affected supply of money in the economy. Banks focused more on collections of loans issued earlier. Banks resulted to cost cutting measures which included staff layoffs and closure of bank branches. The government therefore requires implementing other polices to address the supply of money. On the contrary, according to Muriuki et al. (2017), the profitability of commercial banks in Kenya improved with the interest rate regulation. They further suggested that banks need to reduce bureaucracy or restrictions on the terms of lending to increase the client base and hence interest income.

Alternatively, banks can implement collateral on all loans to reduce exposure to risk. Olukoye and Juma (2017) echoed that approved loans increased since the implementation of caps in Kenya. Other scholars argue that the implementation of interest rate caps led to dire consequences. There was reduced credit supply, witnessed exit of lenders due to high operational costs and risks and an increase in informal lending channels (Wangalwa et al. 2018). This argument motivates the following hypothesis:

H1: Bank profitability is negatively affected by an interest rate policy that imposes restrictions on the cost of lending.

Based on the general hypothesis in H1, we derive the following sub-hypotheses:

H1a: There is a negative association between return on equity and changes in interest rate regulation.
H1b: Net interest margin of banks is negatively associated with changes in interest rate regulation.

According to Nganga and Wanyoike (2017), interest rate is an important macroeconomic variable which directly has an impact on economic growth. Interest rate caps are expected to have a positive impact on stock market performance due to lower cost of capital and increased supply of funds for investment. However, from empirical findings, ceilings on interest rates have a negative impact on stock market performance. There have been dire consequences of capping interest rates on equity markets. Bank stocks in Kenya declined by 25% with the introduction of interest rate caps. Many foreign investors exited the Kenyan equity market as documented by Mawadza (2018). Panda (2008) echoes that the negative relationship between share price and interest rate is purely theoretical.

This argument motivates the following hypothesis:

H2: Kenyan banks should exhibit a decrease in value after interest rate regulation implementation.

4 Methodology

4.1 Analysis of Bank Performance

Several studies have sought to identify factors with which bank performance can be measured. Recent studies on bank performance in the developing economies include Malhotra et al. (2011), Tennant and Tracey (2014) Bakiciol (2017), and Sturn and Zwickl (2015), and Walia and Kaur (2015), Echekoba et al. (2014), and Frederick (2014). The three broad performance categories in banking outlined in the literature are profitability, financial risk, and management efficiency.

Profitability measures include net interest margin, risk-adjusted return on capital, and return on equity. Examples of measures of management efficiency are operating expense ratio, noninterest income as percent of total income, and noninterest expense as percent of revenue. Risk measures are of particular importance, especially from the viewpoint of policy makers and bank regulators. This, as alluded to earlier, is because of the heavy burden that an insolvent bank places on the larger economy. Ultimately, bank failure is a financial loss born by depositors and taxpayers. For this reason, the most important risk measures are those that target capital adequacy. The regulatory goal of capital adequacy, as stipulated by the Basel Committee on Banking Supervision is to ensure that the size of tier 1 capital (common equity) is sufficiently large to absorb unexpected losses. Two important bank-specific risk measures are capital adequacy ratio and equity multiplier ratio. The former divides tier 1 equity capital by the bank's risky assets while the latter is the ratio of interest-earning assets to tier 1 equity capital. A useful operating risk measure is interest rate risk exposure, which divides interest-sensitive assets by interest-sensitive liabilities.

The empirical formulation in this study is an adaptation of the multivariate approach described in Bakiciol (2017). In this study, however, the primary performance metric, designed to capture bank profitability, is net interest margin. The substitute for this metric is net interest income or as specified in Malhotra et al. (2011), interest spread. Over the sample period, this study will attempt to determine whether the introduction and repeal of interest rate ceiling has a material impact on bank profitability. Control variables that will be included as regressors in the model will reflect each bank's degree of risk exposure and level of management efficiency, as described earlier. Financial studies that have utilized these metrics in various empirical analyses on bank performance include Gatsi (2012), Were and Wambua (2014), Walia and Kaur (2015), and more recently, Tarus and Manyala (2018).

4.2 Model Specification

Abstracting from the methodology specified in Malhotra et al. (2011), the following basic model will be used to examine the financial performance of banks:

$$PERF_{it} = \beta_0 + \beta_1 IRS_{it} + \beta_2 MEF_{it} + \beta_3 CAR_{it} + \beta_4 LIQ_{it} + \beta_5 D_{1it} + \beta_6 D_{2it} + \varepsilon_{it}$$

(1)

where PERFit is a measure of bank financial performance for firm i at time t specified as return on equity, net interest margin or Tobin's Q, IRS is interest rate spread, MEF is management efficiency, CAR is capital adequacy ratio, LIQ is liquidity ratio, D1 is the dummy variable for time in which interest rate regulation was introduced, D2 is the dummy variable for time in which interest rate regulation was repealed and ε is the error term

As it turns out, the pooled OLS regression specified in Eq. (1) will not be able to account for the individual characteristics of the different banks. By lumping together different banks at different times, we, in effect, mask any such individuality. Running the regression plain vanilla might therefore lead to regression coefficients that will most likely be biased and inconsistent. To resolve this so-called problem of firm heterogeneity, a fixed-effect regression is preferred. Similar to Platt (2018), a fixed effects model with difference-in-difference (DID) technique will be implemented to highlight the possible impact on bank performance during periods of changes in interest rate policy. Accordingly, the following DID model is specified:

$$PERF_{it} = \beta_0 + \beta_1 D_1 + \beta_2 D_2 + \beta_3 (D_1 \times D_2) + \beta_4 IRS_{it} + \beta_5 MEF_{it} + \beta_6 CAR_{it}$$
$$+ \beta_7 LIQ_{it} + \beta_8 \sum_{t=1}^{n} controls_{it} + \beta_9 D_3 + \omega_{it} + \varepsilon_{it}$$

(2)

where PERFit is bank financial performance for firm i at time t specified as return on equity, net interest margin and Tobin's Q, D1 time period dummy 1 for period 2 observation (post-event), 0 in period 1 (pre-event), D2 for treatment group (TG), 0 for control group (CG), (D1 × D2) interaction dummy variable (equals 1 for observations from TG in Period 2), IRS is interest rate spread, MEF is management efficiency, CAR is capital adequacy ratio, LIQ is liquidity ratio, controls and ε is the error term.

For robustness, to deal with problems of endogeneity (commonly found in panel data), heteroskedasity and serial correlation, two-step generalized methods of moments (GMM) will be adopted. In addition, Hansen J test will be performed to check for the problem of over identification or validity of instruments (Salem et al. 2020).

$$PERF_{it} = \varphi_0 + \varphi_1 PERF_{it-1} + \varphi_2 D_1 + \varphi_3 D_2 + \varphi_4 (D_1 \times D_2) + \varphi_5 IRS_{it}$$
$$+ \varphi_6 MEF_{it} + \varphi_7 CAR_{it} + \varphi_8 LIQ_{it} + \varphi_9 \sum_{t=1}^{n} controls_{jt} + \varphi_{10} D_3 + \omega_{it} + \varepsilon_{it}$$

(3)

where PERFit is bank financial performance specified as return on equity (ROE), net interest margin (NIM), or Tobin Q (TQ), PERFit-1 is first lag of the dependent variable (bank financial performance) which is serves as an internal instrument, D1 is time period dummy 1 for period 2 observation (post-event), 0 in period 1 (pre-event), D2 is dummy for treatment group (TG), 0 for control group (CG), D1 × D2 is interaction dummy variable (equals 1 for observations from TG in Period 2), IRS is interest rate spread,MEF is measure of management efficiency, CAR is capital adequacy ratio (measure of risk exposure), LIQ is liquidity ratio, Controls are gross loans, non-performing loans, total assets, interest expense, GDP and inflation, ω is fixed time effect for year, firm,country and ε is the error term. Variable definitions for both dependent and independent variables in the model are included in the Appendix, Table 3.

4.3 Sample and Data

For the purposes of this study, our dataset covers period 2004–2019 for 78 banks in the five East African countries namely: Kenya, Burundi, Rwanda, Tanzania and Uganda. The period is worth investigating because interest rate caps were imposed in Kenya in 2016 and consequently repealed in 2019. In addition, comparison with other East Africa countries due to similarity in the market. The treatment sample was Kenya while control sample is obtained from Burundi, Rwanda, Tanzania and Uganda that had no changes in interest rate regulation during the period of study. In total we had 1278 observations. The closing period of 2019 is selected owing to the availability of the latest set of audited financial statements for the banks when the study was being conducted.

The specific bank level data is collected from Orbis Bank Focus database and the regulatory data from World Bank database.

5 Results and Discussion

5.1 Bank Performance and Interest Rate Regulation

Table 1 shows the results of the multivariate regression analyses. The dependent variables are return on equity (ROE), net interest margin (NIM) and Tobin's Q (TQ). In order to evaluate the impact of changes in interest rate regulation on banks financial performance, we employ a difference-in-difference methodology, whereby we compare differences in banks financial performance before and after changes in interest rate regulation (interest rate caps) in Kenya and compare those differences with the differences in a control sample of banks from countries that have not been subject to the interest rate regime shift. The impact of the interest rate regulation is therefore measured using an interaction dummy variable (treatment group × post event period) which takes the value of 1 for Kenya/treatment country for years 2016–2019 (post event period after interest rate caps), and 0 otherwise.

The results in Model 1 reveal the interaction dummy variable is positive and significant at the 0.01 level. This implies that changes in interest rate regulation (interest rate caps) increased the return on equity for the treatment group or Kenya. This finding is consistent Muriuki et al. (2017), implies that profitability of banks in Kenya improved with the introduction of interest rate caps. Though, this is contrary to Matundura (2018) argument that interest rate caps reduced profitability for banks in Kenya. Banks reacted to implementation of interest rate caps thorough cost cutting measures like staff layoffs and reduced lending to risky borrowers. This could have increased profitability. In addition, interest rate spread (IRS) is positive and not significant to return on assets. Similarly, management efficiency (MEF) is positive but not significant to return on assets. Capital adequacy ratio (CAR) is negative and significant at the 0.01 level to return on assets. Liquidity ratio (LIQ), regulatory capital (REG) and gross loans (LON) are negative and not significant to return on assets. As expected, non-performing loans (NPL) is negative and significant at the 0.01 level to return on assets while interest expense (INT) was positive and not significant to return on assets. Total assets (TAS) and cost efficiency (COS) are both positive and significant at the 0.05 level to rerun on assets. GDP and inflation (INF) are positive and significant at the 0.01 and 0.05 level respectively.

On the contrary, in Model 2, net interest margin is the dependent variable, the coefficient of the variable of interest, interaction dummy variable is negative and not significant. This implies that changes in interest rate regulation had no impact on NIM. Interest rate spread, non-performing loans and interest expense are positive and significant at the 0.05 level to net interest margin. Management efficiency, capital adequacy ratio and total assets are negative and significantly related net interest margin.

Model 1 and 2 are for return on equity and net interest margin respectively, which are accounting measures of the financial performance. In Model 3, we use market value measure that is, Tobin's Q. The coefficient of the interaction dummy variable is negative and significant at the 0.05 level. Therefore, this implies that investors did not view implementation of interest rate controls to be beneficial. The results support H2 findings are in alignment with Mawadza (2018), that introduction of interest rates caps saw bank stocks and overall market capitalisation decline by 25%. Furthermore, foreign investors exited the Kenyan market upon the introduction of interest rate caps.

Table 1. Difference-in-difference (DID) estimation results

Dependent Variable	ROE	NIM	TQ
Model	[1]	[2]	[3]
constant	8.663**(−1.78)	8.294***(5.70)	−14.579**(−2.13)
Interaction dummy variable	4.078***(3.72)	−0.341(−1.04)	−2.924**(−1.88)
irs	2.978(1.58)	1.012**(1.82)	−2.230(−0.70)
mef	0.575(0.57)	−0.907***(−3.02)	14.399***(7.00)
car	−0.088***(−2.79)	−0.024**(−2.52)	0.006(0.08)
liq	−33.156(−0.70)	21.820(1.55)	−336.996(−1.14)
reg	−0.145(−0.27)	−0.040(−0.26)	11.109**(1.90)
lon	−0.395(−0.79)	−0.116(−0.78)	0.357(0.45)
npl	−0.112***(−3.95)	0.015**(1.81)	0.002(0.03)
int	0.039(1.08)	0.023**(2.15)	−0.030(−1.11)

(*continued*)

Table 1. (*continued*)

Dependent Variable	ROE	NIM	TQ
Model	[1]	[2]	[3]
tas	0.003**(2.35)	−0.001**(−1.76)	0.001(0.64)
cos	8.761**(2.19)	1.431(1.20)	−1.103(−0.22)
gdp	0.584***(4.08)	0.041(0.95)	0.215(1.16)
infl	0.890**(2.15)	0.049(0.40)	0.684(1.30)
Hausman	450.98	30.28	50.82
chi-square(χ2)	0.000	0.000	0.000
F statistic	9.61	2.49	5.23
P value	0.000	0.000	0.000
Adjusted R-square	0.579	0.764	0.629
Firm fixed effects	Yes	Yes	Yes
Year fixed effects	Yes	Yes	Yes
Sample size	1278	1278	304
No. of banks	78	78	19

Note *, ** and *** denote significance at the 10, 5 and 1% respectively; t values are in parentheses

5.2 Robustness Checks

We run a robustness check to control for potential endogeneity that is common in panel data by performing two-step generalized methods of moments (GMM) estimation. The results are shown in Table 2. Overall, we find the interaction variable to be positive and significant to return on equity. This is as reported in the previous section. This evidence is not in support of H1a which denotes that there is a negative relationship between changes in interest rate regulation (implementation of interest rate caps) return on equity and Model 2 results shows that the difference or coefficient is negative but not significant to net interest margin which is similar to results in Table 1.

Interestingly, the results in Model 3 show that Tobin Q has a positive and not significant interaction dummy variable. This is contrary to results in Table 1. This implies that implementation of interest rate caps had a positive impact on the investors. This calls for further analysis on this. We perform Hansen's test to ensure the instrumented variables are not over-identified and the results show validity to this effect.

Table 2. Generalised Method of Moments (GMM) estimation results

Dependent Variable	ROE	NIM	TQ
Model	[1]	[2]	[3]
Interaction dummy variable	3.379***(2.82)	−0.115(−0.27)	0.134(0.14)
irs	10.404**(1.79)	5.750**(2.04)	−5.668**(−2.40)
mef	−0.503(−0.55)	−1.078**(−2.51)	−8.585(−1.58)
car	−0.079***(−3.21)	−0.025***(−3.12)	−0.032(−0.77)
liq	93.838**(1.83)	−15.094(−0.85)	395.99**(2.22)
reg	−0.746(−1.19)	0.705***(2.96)	−6.607**(−2.06)
lon	2.634***(8.15)	0.103(0.83)	−0.151(−0.37)
npl	−0.177***(−5.05)	0.025**(2.54)	−0.043(−1.05)
int	−0.110***(−4.83)	−0.020**(1.85)	0.009(1.16)
tas	0.003***(4.82)	0.001**(2.39)	0.000(0.43)
cos	5.223**(1.89)	8.965***(7.93)	4.835(1.15)
gdp	0.286**(1.95)	0.024(0.47)	0.120(0.90)
infl	1.016**(2.13)	0.423***(3.01)	−0.476(−1.54)
No. of parameters	15	15	15
No.of moments	16	16	16
Hansen J's $\chi 2$	0.60	17.75	6.75
Sample size	1278	1278	304
No. of banks	78	78	19

Note *, ** and *** denote significance at the 10, 5 and 1% respectively; t values are in parentheses

6 Conclusion

This study assessed the effect of interest rate regulation on banks financial performance in Kenya. The study utilized balanced panel data of 78 banks from five countries in East Africa over the period, 2004–2019. We examine both accounting and market measures of bank performance, namely: return on equity, net interest margin and Tobin Q.

The multivariate analyses show a positive and significant coefficient, therefore financial performance, that is, return on equity increased after the implementation of interest rate caps in Kenya. Though the impact on net interest margin was insignificant. Similarly, interest rate caps impact on the value of listed banks was insignificant. The results, in combination with existing literature suggest that the increase in banks profitability may be due to reductions in operating expenses, lending to more risky borrowers especially SMEs and an increase in non-interest income especially transaction fees.

Our results are relevant given that Central Bank of Kenya continually regulates interest rates charged by commercial banks. In addition, this study contributes to other policy makers in East Africa region who want to consider implementation of interest rate caps to regulate the lending interest rates. In addition, the results are bridging the gap between theory and practice regarding the impact of interest rate controls.

Further research might concentrate on the larger Sub-Saharan region. GMM results showed that changes in interest rate regulations had a positive and not significant impact on the stock market. There is need for further analysis on this.

Appendix

Table 3. Variable definitions

Category	Variables	Measurement or Ratio Used	Source
Dependent variables	ROE	Net Income / Equity Capital	Orbis Bank Focus data
	NIM	Interest Income-Interest Expense Interest earning assets	Orbis Bank Focus data
	Tobin Q	(Number of outstanding shares x price) + book value of total assets −book value of equity / Book value of assets	Orbis Bank Focus data, specific country stock exchange
Independent variables	Interest rate spread	Average lending interest rate-average deposit interest rate	Orbis Bank Focus data
	Management efficiency	Total advances / Total assets	Orbis Bank Focus data
	Capital adequacy ratio	Equity capital / Risky assets	Orbis Bank Focus data
	Liquidity risk ratio	Liquid assets / Total assets	Orbis Bank Focus data
Control variables	GDP	Annual real GDP growth	World Bank
	Inflation	Annual inflation	World Bank

References

Akerlof, G.: The market for "Lemons": quality and uncertainty and the market mechanism. Q. J. Econ. **84**(3), 488–500 (1970)

Atiti, F., Agung, R., Kimani, S.: Competition and Banking Sector Stability in Kenya, KBA Centre for Research on Financial Markets and Policy. Working paper series 41, Nairobi (2020)

Aglionby, J.: Shares in Kenyan bank hit after Interest Rates Cap move. Financial Times (2016)

Allen, L.: The determinants of bank interest margins: a note. J. Financ. Quant. Anal. 23(2), 231–235 (1998)

Allen, F., Gale, D.: Financial intermediaries and markets. Econometrica 72(4), 1023–1061 (2004)

Alper, C.E., Clements, B., Hobdari, N., Porcel, R.M.: Do interest rate controls? Evidence from Kenya. Rev. Dev. Econ. 24(3), 910–926 (2019)

Amidu, M.: Bank competition in Africa: do institutional quality and cross-border banking matter? J. Afr. Bus. 20(4), 1–35 (2020)

Bakiciol, T.: The impact of durable relationship with banks when crisis hits. Emerg. Mark. Financ. Trade 53(11), 2609–2624 (2017)

Central Bank of Kenya: The Impact of Interest Rate Capping on the Kenyan Economy, Discussion paper (2018). https://www.centralbank.go.ke/wp-content/uploads/2018/03/Interest-Rate-Caps_-March-2018final.pdf

Diamond, D.W.: Financial intermediation and delegated monitoring. Rev. Econ. Stud. 51(3), 393–414 (1984)

Echekoba, F.N., Egbunike, C.F., Ezu, G.K.: Determinants of bank profitability in Nigeria: using camel rating model (2001–2010). IOSR J. Bus. Manag. 16(9), 44–50 (2014)

Flamini, V., Schumacher, M.L., McDonald, M.C.A.: The Determinants of Commercial Bank Profitability in Sub-Saharan Africa. International Monetary Fund (2009)

Frederick, N.K.: Factors affecting performance of commercial banks in Uganda: a case for domestic commercial banks. In: Proceedings of 25th International Business Research Conference, South Africa (2014). ISBN 978-1-922069-42-9

Gatsi, J.G.: Capital structure of Ghanaian banks: an evaluation of its impact on performance. IUP J. Bank Manag. 11(4), 86–99 (2012)

Kavwele, D.T., Ariemba, J.M., Evusa, Z.: Effect of interest rate capping on the financial performance of commercial banks in Kenya. Int. J. Bus. Manag. Econ. Res. 9(1), 1182–1190 (2018)

Leland, H., Pyle, D.: Informational asymmetries, financial structure and financial intermediation. J. Financ. 32, 371–387 (1977)

Malhotra, D.K., Poteau, R., Singh, R.: Evaluating the performance of commercial banks in India. Asia Pac. J. Financ. Bank. Res. 5(5), 15–37 (2011)

Matundura, E.: The effects of capping interest rate on profitability of Kenya commercial bank. J. Econ. Financ. 9(2), 34–37 (2018)

Mawadza, C.: Interest Rate Caps: An International Perspective, World Bank Group Presentation. Winter School (2018)

Mdoe, I.J., Omolo, J.O., Wawire, N.H.: Bank competition in Kenya. J. Ind. Compet. Trade 19(1), 83–102 (2013). https://doi.org/10.1007/s10842-018-0279-2

Mdoe, I.J., Omolo, J.O., Wawire, N.H.: Bank competitive landscape and competition in the banking sector in Kenya. Afr. Rev. Econ. Financ. 11(1), 220–251 (2019)

Muriuki, F., Mathuva, E., Egondi, P.: Influence of interest rate capping on financial performance of commercial banks in Mombasa County, Kenya. Imperial J. Interdisc. Res. 3(9), 959–966 (2017)

Nganga, R., Wanyoike, M.: The effect of interest rate control on the stock market performance, a case of Nairobi securities exchange market. Int. J. Curr. Aspects Finan. 4(1), 48–54 (2017)

Ngugi, R.: An empirical analysis of interest rate spread, African Economic Research Consortium Research paper 106, Nairobi, AERC (2001)

Olukoye, B., Juma, D.: Effect of interest rate capping policy on financial performance of commercial banks in Kenya: case of equity bank Kenya limited in Nairobi county. Int. J. Sci. Res. 7(11), 481–486 (2017)

Ombongi, P.N., Long, W.: Assessing nature of competition in Kenya's banking sector. Int. J. Res. Bus. Stud. Manag. **5**(2), 11–19 (2018)

Panda, C.: Do interest rates matter for stock markets? Econ. Polit. Wkly. **43**(17), 107–115 (2008)

Platt, K.: European Union enlargement announcement and corporate valuations. Emerg. Markets Finan. Trade **43**(2), 430–449 (2018)

Safavian, M., Zia, B.: The Impact of Interest Rate Caps on the Financial Sector: Evidence from Commercial Banks in Kenya. Policy Research Working Paper 8393, World Bank Group (2018)

Salem, R., Usman, M., Ezeani, E.: Loan loss provisions and audit quality: evidence from MENA islamic and conventional banks. Q. Rev. Econ. Finan. **79**, 345–359 (2020)

Sharpe, S.: Asymmetric information, bank lending and implicit contracts: a stylized model of customer relationships. J. Financ. **45**(4), 1069–1087 (1990)

Sturn, S., Zwickl, K.: A reassessment of intermediation and size effects of financial systems. Empirical Econ. **50**, 1467–1480 (2015)

Tarus, D.K., Manyala, P.O.: What determines bank interest rate spread? Evidence from Sub-Saharan Africa. Afr. J. Econ. Manag. Stud. **9**(3), 335–348 (2018)

Tennant, D.F., Tracey, M.R.: Financial intermediation and stock market volatility in a small bank dominated economy. J. Dev. Areas **48**(4), 73–95 (2014)

Walia, K., Kaur, P.: Performance evaluation of the Indian banking sector: a study of selected commercial banks. IUP J. Bank Manag. **14**(2), 38–48 (2015)

Wangalwa, H.H., Kahuthia, J., Ndegwa, J.: Strategic responses to interest rates capping by central bank of Kenya and its effect on financial performance on commercial banks in Kenya. Strateg. J. Bus. Change Manag. **5**(3), 640–647 (2018)

Were, M., Wambua, J.: What factors drive interest rate spread of commercial banks? Empirical evidence from Kenya. Rev. Dev. Financ. **4**, 73–82 (2014)

Towards an API Marketplace
for an e-Invoicing Ecosystem

Chinmay Manchanda[1,3]([✉]) [iD], Walayat Hussain[2] [iD], Latif Rabhi[3],
and Fethi Rabhi[1,3] [iD]

[1] School of Computer Science and Engineering, UNSW, Sydney, Australia
c.manchanda@student.unsw.edu.au
[2] Peter Faber Business School, Australian Catholic University, North Sydney,
Australia
walayat.hussain@acu.edu.au
[3] Ebusiness Software Services, Sydney, Australia
http://ebsoftwareservices.com.au/

Abstract. Driven by a large number of very diverse and fast-evolving
regulations, the adoption of e-invoicing is creating many challenges for
solution providers, such as dealing with compliance requirements, cross-
border issues, heterogeneity of standards and constant changes. Existing
solutions do not represent a cost-effective and vendor-independent alternative to existing legacy systems, ERPs and databases. The proposed
solution is based on leveraging cloud computing concepts, Software-as-a-
Service concept, API economy, and Business Process Modelling (BPM)
concepts. It allows solution providers to choose SaaS components and
customise their offerings according to customers needs. Given an ecosystem of APIs available via a marketplace, it becomes possible to rapidly
compose and build new applications via BPM technologies. The paper
describes an implementation of this concept realised using several e-
invoicing APIs being composed using the WASP workflow system. Some
preliminary results regarding the feasibility of the proposed approach in
a simple buyer-seller scenario are discussed.

Keywords: e-invoicing · Industry 4.0 · API · SaaS · WASP · UBL ·
PEPPOL

1 Introduction

The "digitisation" of production and logistics provides many significant, new
advantages to modern supply chain management in the so-called Industry 4.0
concept. Design features of Industry 4.0 are interoperability, virtualisation,
decentralisation, quick response, service orientation and modularity. This paper
is concerned with document exchanges to facilitate collaboration between business partners and, in particular, e-invoicing.

Regulations play an important role in adopting e-invoicing within one country or region. Such regulations mandate the use of certain standards to guarantee

the security and integrity of business document exchanges and fight against tax evasion and fraud. For example, the EU Commission implemented in April 2014 new regulations relating to public procurement across Europe in the form of the e-invoicing Directive 2014/55/EU, which sets out deadlines by which European government bodies must be able to receive structured electronic invoices from suppliers. The introduction of e-invoicing legislation across Europe in particular has greatly boosted the number of companies wishing to be able to exchange structured electronic invoices. Currently the number of invoices sent across Europe annually is estimated to exceed 40 billion. Meanwhile, the annual growth rate for e-invoicing is around 10–20%.

Although, e-invoicing has enabled businesses to efficiently generate e-bills and track them in real-time to reduce the possibilities of fraud and avoid any data entry errors. However, e-invoicing is creating many challenges, such as compliance, cross-border issues, data heterogeneity, changeable rules and regulations, and the identification of errors in complex systems. Compliance issues arise when different regulations within each country change very quickly. For example, in France, medium companies must use e-invoicing by 1 July 2025 and small companies by 1 July 2026. Rules and regulations differ from country to country and even region within countries. Some countries and states within one country impose additional requirements such as archiving and e-reporting, which can be tricky to implement, raising additional issues related to compliance of cross-border transactions. The issue of heterogeneity arises when the system deals with various data and messaging standards and formats, particularly when messages need to be sent via different delivery protocols (hub, Web Service, PEPPOL). Moreover, error handling is another big issue in e-invoicing. Systems with a high degree of complexity and automation mean errors are very hard to detect and correct in a timely fashion.

The paper proposes creating an e-invoicing ecosystem of services to address these challenges. The proposed system can be composed, configured, and customised according to different contexts under Service-Oriented Architecture (SOA) and Business Process Modelling (BPM) principles [18]. We demonstrate this idea through a pilot case study on the rapid development of an e-invoicing application using existing services and a workflow engine.

The paper is structured as follows. Section 2 presents some background and related work on e-invoicing discussing the standards in place. Section 3 describes our solution and Sect. 3.4 an implementation using the WASP worflow portal. Section 4 describes some preliminary evaluation results and Sect. 5 concludes this paper.

2   Related Work

We first describe the area of e-invoicing with its main drivers and challenges. This is followed by an overview of existing standards and solutions. In the next section, we review existing efforts that can lead to opportunities to deliver efficient e-invoices services via API marketplaces.

2.1   e-Invoicing Drivers and Barriers

Electronic invoicing (e-invoicing) enables businesses to exchange digital invoices in a safe, efficient and secure manner through software without the intervention of humans. E-invoicing depends on secure networks and opens common data standards that enables software to exchange business information seamlessly and automatically [13].

The drivers and challenges associated with the adoption of e-invoicing are illustrated in several publications. For example, [16] runs 3 case studies and observes the drivers and barriers to the adoption of e-invoicing in large scale Greek manufacturing industries. The main drivers are acceleration of invoicing process, reduced costs and improved auditing and compliance with tax rules and regulations. The barriers related to navigating through complex regulations and costs are caused by changes to existing IT infrastructure to adapt to standards.

[12] states that although the benefits associated with the adoption of e-invoicing have been highlighted in numerous reports and international forums, the adoption rate in most countries has not reached 20%. The firm must perceive the benefits derived from e-invoicing both before and after adopting the IT and communication infrastructure since they have a positive and significant influence on the firm's behaviour. Perceived security is also necessary for a firm to use e-invoicing for the first time. Nevertheless, once adoption has taken place, this factor no longer influences the user's intentions. Therefore, security cannot be considered a differentiating aspect of e-invoicing but, rather, an indispensable and inherent characteristic. Finally, ease of use will increase intentions of continuing to use e-invoicing among firms that have already adopted it. It accelerates the learning process and means that the benefits obtained will be more highly valued.

The two main barriers inhibiting the growth of e-invoicing are systems issues and supplier reluctance [1]. The Basware study found that companies' reasons for engaging in e-invoicing include improved processes, increased accuracy, and lower costs. Those that implemented e-invoicing most frequently cited foster transactions, improved processes, greater accuracy, and improved compliance and audits as key benefits they have achieved. Improved customer service and supplier relations were also mentioned as benefits. One reason for the low adoption rate is that the business world is riddled with legacy systems. For instance, many companies have multiple systems for ordering, accounting, and paying and are still struggling to get these internal systems to communicate with each other, let alone with all their suppliers' different systems. For these reasons, many standards have emerged to facilitate interoperability at different levels (e.g. data, transport, business process).

2.2   e-Invoicing Standards and Solutions

As mentioned earlier, the European Parliament and Council defined a common standard for e-invoicing named Directive 2014/55/EU to provide a common template to develop interoperability within the European Union [6]. This has triggered the development of several standards, one of which is a common business term dictionary or data model (the European Norm EN16931[1]). Where necessary, however, countries or organisations can create a separate Core Invoice Usage Specification (CIUS). For example, XRechnung is a Core Invoice Usage Specification (CIUS) of the EN 16931 used in Germany. In addition to the data model, message representation standards are based on notations such as XML. For example, there are two supported XML formats of XRechnung (as with the EN 16931). The first one is CII (UN/CEFACT Cross Industry Invoice). The second one (from Oasis Open) is the evolution of an older standard [19] called UBL 2.x ISO/IEC 19845 in 2015[2].

In addition, Germany also uses the ZUGFeRD 2.1 standard for hybrid invoicing (in France, the same standard is referred to as Factor-X). This standard uses a human-readable PDF/A3 invoice document in which a CII invoice is embedded. The e-invoicing format used in Spain is FacturaE, an XML-based invoice format that uses e-signatures and follows the XAdES standard. Italy also uses an XML standard format called InvoicePA with two digital signature formats: CAdES-BES (CMS) and XAdES-BES (XML).

In 2014, the European Commission declared that UBL 2.1 was officially eligible for referencing tenders from public administrations (one of the first non-European standards recognised). It is expected that the adoption of UBL as a standard message representation will increase as it defines a royalty-free library of standard XML business documents that not only supports invoicing but also all other aspects related to the digitisation of the commercial and logistical processes for domestic and international supply chains (e.g. procurement, purchasing, transport, logistics, intermodal freight management).

In addition to data and messaging standards, there are multiple alternatives for communicating invoices:

- Centralised system: in which invoices can be uploaded and transferred via file transfer protocols or web services. This is the most common method for B2G exchanges such as PPF (formerly Chorus-Pro) in France. However, there are exceptions. For example, in Italy, all invoices, including B2B, have been exchanged via Sistema di Interscambio (SdI) from 1 January 2019.
- 2-corner model: supplier and buyer exchange invoices directly via a private network (e.g. EDIFACT) or email but the latter is less common as there are no guarantees of delivery.
- 4-corner model: supplier and buyer exchange invoices via Accredited Service Providers that provide the required connection to a network. This is the model used in the PEPPOL network, described next.

PEPPOL [7] is a set of artifacts and technical specifications which facilitate easy data exchange across disparate government systems and their suppliers. Many EU countries have adopted PEPPOL[3] as a communication method,

---

[1] https://www.en-standard.eu/.

[2] https://www.oasis-open.org/committees/tc_home.php?wg_abbrev=ubl.

[3] PEPPOL most recent usage statistics in can be accessed at PEPPOL statistics from ionite.net.

including Belgium, Croatia, Cyprus, Denmark, Greece, Ireland, Latvia, Lithuania, Luxemburg, Malta, Norway, Poland, Slovenia, Sweden and the UK[4].

In addition to communication protocols, there are various business processes (involving different business entities) that can be used to exchange invoices. These business processes depend on the type of e-invoicing (B2G, B2B, B2C), the application domain, the communication method used (hub, 2-corner, 4-corner), and the business's nature relationship. For example, UBL defines several business processes that can be used to exchange invoices, such as pre-payment, spot payment, payment in advance of delivery, invoices with references to despatch advice, etc.

Besides e-invoicing, there are now a number of e-reporting requirements being introduced. For example, the French tax authorities are discussing defining a lifecycle for e-invoices, e.g. created, rejected, paid etc. Changes in status of an e-invoice must be reported to tax authorities alongside other data. PEPPOL is also introducing the capacity for service providers to do e-reporting (the so-called 5-corner model). There are many ongoing standardisation efforts: CEN/TC 440 [10], which consolidates standardisation efforts in several supply chain processes, including electronic ordering, tendering, notification, and fulfilment across 14 business sectors.

Many e-invoicing solutions come under a variety of forms to address the challenges of implementing these standards, such as:

– Enterprise systems: e-invoicing functionalities are integrated within a large enterprise system such as IBM or SAP, providing all necessary functions behind the scene.
– Accounting systems: similarly, e-invoicing functionalities are integrated within an accounting application such as Xero or MYOB.
– E-Invoicing systems: complete e-invoicing solution which can be customised to different data formats, and delivery protocols, offering all functions to be integrated with a local information system or ERP. Examples include Pagero.

Whilst these solutions are suitable for Government agencies and large companies, they present difficulties when adopted by SMEs, namely high cost, lack of flexibility and vendor lock-in.

As a result, we believe that there is a need for cost-effective solutions that are both open and flexible to allow companies to better leverage their existing assets.

3 Proposed Solution

3.1 Towards an API Marketplace for e-Invoicing Services

The proposed solution is based on leveraging the concepts of cloud computing, Software-as-a-Service concept, API economy and Business Process Modelling (BPM). These are explained briefly next.

---

[4] https://ecosio.com/en/white-paper-e-invoicing-in-europe/.

Cloud computing is the primary delivery vehicle for a new generation of software services referred to as Software-as-a-Service (SaaS). Essentially the in-infrastructure and software are no longer on "premise" and the SaaS provider supplies the network access, security, application software, and data storage from a server. On a technical level, any SaaS functionality is delivered via an Application Programmable Interface (or API) accessible through a web browser, mobile device, or another application. These APIs are developed according to four key factors; necessity, reliability, usability, and scalability. SaaS charging models are generally aligned with the fact that users pay for what they use rather than paying a high upfront standardised cost regardless of their usage. One key target market for the SaaS model is small to medium-sized businesses [3], as it lowers entry costs. Providers can use a range of charging models such as perpetual licence, subscription, transaction-based, and ad-funded. In Information Systems (IS) research, APIs are conceptualised and analysed as boundary resources, i.e., resources at the interface between platform owners and third-party developers [3].

The SaaS model has enabled the emergence of *API marketplaces* which provide a place for developers to build and share their APIs and a consumer to find a suitable API for integration into their applications[5]. Such marketplaces exist (e.g. Rapid API), but many researchers pointed out that it is not a trivial job for a consumer to find suitable APIs from a myriad of APIs in a constantly growing and evolving API landscape [17,22,24]. Multiple studies have attempted to address the issue by exploring the relationship between consumers, APIs and consumers with APIs for optimal recommendations [9,23,25]. Chen et al. [5] proposed an API recommendation model using a deep learning method that aggregated the text details in source code with the API usage by API Context Graph Network and Code Token Network. Authors found that combing textual code details improve the accuracy. In a similar approach, Qi et al. [21] proposed a text description-driven web API recommendation that assures the suggested API's compatibility using mashup creation records. Lian and Tang [14] proposed an API recommendation method using a graph collaborative filtering method that identifies the relationship between a consumer and an API. The authors experimented using a real dataset from Programmableweb.com and found that the approach performed better than other approaches.

The availability of APIs makes it possible to rapidly compose them and build new applications via business process modelling (BPM) principles and technologies. BPM can be categorised as any process modelling that is performed to enhance the overall operation of a business, a way to understand and optimise workflows and create data-driven visual representations of key business processes [2]. A BPM language allows the definition of a graphical representation of a business process or workflow that includes attributes such as events that occur within a workflow, who owns and starts those activities, decision points and different paths workflows can take based on their outcomes, devices involved, a timeline of each step and success and failure rates of the process. According

---

[5] https://www.akana.com/blog/api-economy.

to Penker [8] a business process model may have six different reasons to be created, which are: to understand the key mechanisms of an existing business; to orient the creation of suitable information systems that support the business; to implement improvements in the current business; to show the structure of an innovated business; to experiment new business concepts; and to identify business elements not considered part of the core, which could be delegated to an outside supplier [20].

BPMN, the most popular business process modelling language[6] provides a standardised graphical notation that is easy to use for business analysts, allowing them to document and communicate their business processes within their company and external business partners. For more details about BPMN, see [4]. Several open-source and commercial tools support BPM, such as Signavio, Camunda and Kissflow. The availability of these tools is used as a basis for our solution described next.

3.2 Proposed Architecture

As illustrated in Fig. 1, the proposed architecture has the following components:

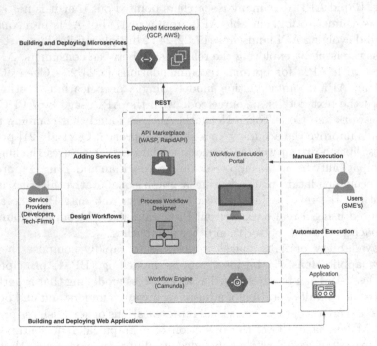

Fig. 1. Proposed Architecture

---

[6] https://www.trisotech.com/bpmn-introduction-and-history/.

- Workflow Engine: This component is the core for controlling all e-invoicing processes. It executes all process instances and their activities as well as the communication with component services invoked via their API.
- Process Workflow Designer: this allows the user to define and manage processes graphically. Such processes are based on the BPMN 2.0 standard.
- Workflow Control Portal: this component allows the user to control workflow instances creation, execution, and monitoring.
- API Marketplace: a marketplace in which several APIs offer functionality that can be integrated into service in the workflow.

This architecture supports two types of users, service providers and end-users (typically SMEs). Service providers consist of developers and technology providers whose aim is to create a range of e-invoicing services. Once deployed, they advertise these services, as mentioned earlier, as APIs in the workflow marketplace.

End-users that are part of companies involved in e-invoicing exchanges will collaboratively design and form certain workflows by combining different services in a logical flow. One example is a seller that uses a workflow supporting the sequence of invoice creation, validation and sending with special cases, e.g. receiving a notification if the invoice is malformed. These workflows, once designed are run on a workflow engine. This engine is responsible for calling the linked services and following the flow. Compared to controlling the flow using a bespoke application, end-users benefit from rapid deployment and modification of workflow (this is important in a fast-changing environment). In addition, these workflows can be executed and simulated manually using the workflow execution portal and/or using automated triggers set up using the web application. Finally, the workflow web portal serves as a third party between the user and the workflow engine and provides the user with human-readable updates on the processes.

3.3   Definition of the Case Study

We define a case study that will be used to drive the implementation of a prototype based on a realistic e-invoicing scenario. We have the simple case of a buyer and a seller in this case study. The seller's responsibilities are:

- Create an invoice in the format expected by the buyer. We assume that the seller has a legacy system that uses EDIFACT, and the buyer requires invoices in UBL to be sent over the PEPPOL network. The seller must check that invoices do not contain an error before sending them.
- The seller must monitor the status of the invoice (see Fig. 2 showing invoice status changes) after it has been sent.

The Buyer's responsibilities are:

- Read the invoice and check there are no errors

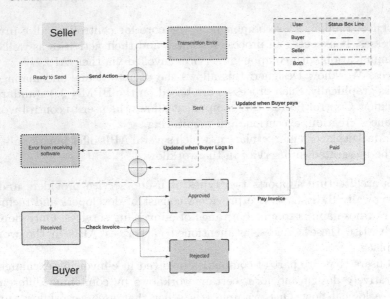

Fig. 2. How invoice status changes during an exchange

- Verify if the invoice should be Rejected or Approved based on the invoice contents.
- Pay the invoice

This process simplifies real-life e-invoicing processes that can include many more statuses and other participants besides a single seller and buyer but will be sufficient to demonstrate the usefulness of the proposed architecture. As an example, Table 1 represents the seller's dashboard in which Inv_2 was sent to the buyer. Table 2 represents the buyer dashboard in a scenario where the buyer has approved the contents of this invoice and will now proceed to pay it using the "Pay" workflow action.

Table 1. Seller Dashboard after sending an invoice

Seller Dashboard							
Invoice Name	Date/Time Uploaded	Sender	Input Document Type	Receiver	Output Document Type	Status	Action
Inv_1	11/5/22 2:27pm	ESS	EDIFACT	UNSW	UBL	Ready to send	Send
Inv_2	11/5/22 2:28pm	ESS	EDIFACT	AWO	UBL	Sent	Send

Table 2. Buyer Dashboard after approving an invoice

Buyer Dashboard							
Invoice Name	Date/Time Uploaded	Sender	Input Document Type	Receiver	Output Document Type	Status	Action
Inv_2	11/5/22 3:28pm	ESS	EDIFACT	AWO	UBL	Approved	Pay

3.4 Implementation

Many ongoing research efforts propose comprehensive workflow development and management platforms such as IceCore[7]. In this implementation, we chose to use the Workflow and Service Automation Platform (WASP)[8] provided via the EFPF Portal[9] as a basis for our implementation.

Five e-invoicing services have been made available to workflow designers through the WASP marketplace:

- Get Pending Messages to Send: this allows messages to be retrieved from the ERP for a particular customer (a seller). It creates an invoice in the UBL XML standard and sends it over the PEPPOL network
- Create and send Invoice: this allows an invoice to be created in the destination format and sent over the relevant network.
- Check status: Checks the status of a message that has been sent
- Retrieve received messages: allows messages to be retrieved from the network for a particular customer (a buyer)
- Set status: allows the status of a message to be changed

Two workflows are designed via WASP Designer: one for the seller and one for the buyer. A snapshot of the seller workflow is shown in Fig. 3.

The first task in this workflow is to create and send the message containing the invoice. This service itself performs multiple tasks like format conversion, checking for errors in the format, validation rules, etc. If the invoice has some errors, the user is notified. Otherwise, the invoice is sent. From that point, the user can check the changes in the status of the invoice until it gets rejected or paid. The buyer has a similar workflow that checks for received invoices and then offers the user the possibility to perform actions such as Approve, Reject or Pay the invoice.

---

[7] https://www.academia.edu/67988083/IceCore_A_Web_Portal_for_Workflow_Execution.
[8] https://www.efpf.org/post/orchestration-workflow-and-service-automation-platform.
[9] https://www.efpf.org/.

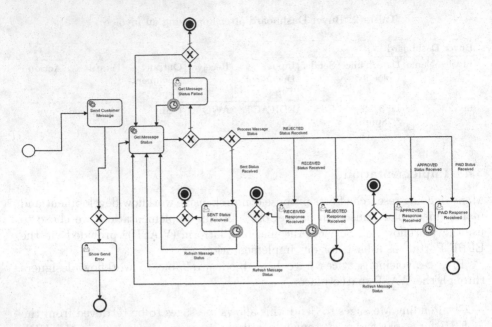

Fig. 3. BPMN Workflow for Send Invoice

4   Evaluation

4.1   Running the Workflows

Running the workflows is conducted via the WASP platform. Users can access and create instances of different processes using the control panel as shown in Fig. 4. Here we can see that the process Send Invoice v5 is started using the actions tab on the right.

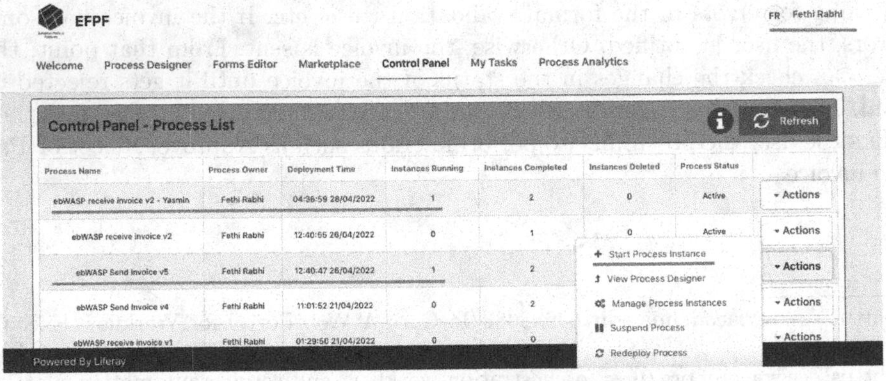

Fig. 4. WASP Control Panel

Upon the execution of the process instance, the task assignee is required to complete the user actions required for the completion of the process. The seller is also presented with a confirmation tab which is displayed to make sure that all the user information is correct and gives the seller an option to complete the said process by using the confirm button, as shown in Fig. 5.

Customer_Name	ESS
Filename	invoice-message-16.txt
messageId	16
DateTime_Uploaded	22/04/2022 11:36
messageType	EDIFACT message
sender	ESS
inDocType	INVOIC D96A
receiver	AWO
outDocType	UBL Invoice ANZ
Message_Status	READY TO SEND

ebWASP – Confirm Message Send
Please Confirm that you wish to send the Message

○ Confirm   ○ Restart - Go back to the 'Enter   ○ Terminate
                        Customer Name' Task.   the Process

Finish

Fig. 5. Confirmation pop up

For the buyer, "My Tasks" panel would contain different actions which will have the impact of changing invoices statuses and triggering other actions. For example, approving the invoice will have the impact of triggering the action of paying invoices. These actions will result in the display status action on the seller side to display the latest status of the invoice.

4.2   Discussion

The prototype implementation has confirmed that the use of an API marketplace combined with the power of BPM technology gives the flexibility for solution providers to rapidly select relevant APIs and form workflows based on the needs of their customers.

There are still many limitations in the proposed approach. Firstly, the creation of workflows still require technical skills and existing workflow portals need to enable business users more control over the creation and execution of their workflows without IT support. Secondly, the number of e-invoicing APIs is still very low so there is a need for e-invoicing authorities to encourage the creation of API marketplaces e.g. via API standardisatrion and accreditation processes.

In addition, the business processes selected in the case study are very simplified versions of those used in reality. There are many more variations such as invoicing of deliveries of goods and services against purchase orders, based on a contract, invoicing the delivery of an incidental purchase order, pre-payment, spot payment, payment in advance of delivery, invoices with references to a dispatch advice etc. Many of the business processes listed above require the use of additional services which either utilise the information produced by one of the services above or sends information to them in order to produce an end result, hence forming a new workflow.

5   Conclusion and Future Work

This paper has reviewed recent developments in the area of e-invoicing and has shown that as e-invoicing processes will mature amongst trading partners, the demand from customers will increase and the entry costs to adopt e-invoicing will be reduced. However, due to the multitude of fast evolving standards and regulations, maintaining such infrastructures will be costly in the long run.

The availability of cloud-based software, storage, and computing resources without upfront infrastructure costs or high fixed costs is becoming an attractive solution for developers to deliver and monetise specialised and customisable solutions to a group of clients with specific needs [11]. Our paper advocates the use of ecosystem of SaaS components for the rapid composition of e-invoicing solutions. Although this idea has been used in different application areas (e.g. [4,15], this paper is first one to suggest its use in e-invoicing.

In the short term, future work will focus on improving the existing prototype to include a realistic business process that gives visibility on all invoice status changes required by existing French tax regulations[10]. In the long term, the ecosystem should be extended to include more services that play a broader role in e-invoicing such as PDF invoice fields recognition, integration with public tax authorities portals, integration with accounting systems etc.

Acknowledgements. We wish to thank eBusiness eXpert and the WASP team for their contributions in developing the case study as part of the ebWASP project. This project/initiative has received funding from the European Union's Horizon 2020 research and innovation programme under grant agreement No. 825075 – EFPF project.

References

1. Overcome the barriers to e-invoicing. IOMA's Report on Managing Accounts Payable **11**(3), 1–11 (2011). https://login.wwwproxy1.library.unsw.edu.au/login?url=https://search.ebscohost.com/login.aspx?direct=true&db=buh&AN=60304555&site=ehost-live&scope=site
2. Anonymous: A Pragmatic Guide to Business Process Modelling. BCS Learning & Development Limited, London, 2nd edn. (2009). https://login.wwwproxy1.library.unsw.edu.au/login?url=https://www.proquest.com/books/1-introduction/docview/189251881/se-2?accountid=12763. Copyright - Copyright British Informatics Society Ltd. 2009. Accessed 13 Sept 2021

---

[10] https://portail.dgfip.finances.gouv.fr/.

3. Bondel, G., Landgraf, A., Matthes, F.: API management patterns for public, partner, and group web API initiatives with a focus on collaboration. In: 26th European Conference on Pattern Languages of Programs. EuroPLoP 2021. Association for Computing Machinery, New York (2021). https://doi.org/10.1145/3489449.3490012

4. Bourr, K., Corradini, F., Pettinari, S., Re, B., Rossi, L., Tiezzi, F.: Disciplined use of BPMN for mission modeling of multi-robot systems. Proc. ISSN **1613**, 0073 (2021). http://ceur-ws.org

5. Chen, C., et al.: Holistic combination of structural and textual code information for context based API recommendation. IEEE Trans. Softw. Eng. 1 (2021). https://doi.org/10.1109/TSE.2021.3074309

6. Dobrzeniecka, E., Możdżyński, D.: Process analysis of implementing structured electronic invoice at the Poznań city hall as an example of process electronisation at public administration units. Inf. Syst. Manage. **7**(1) (2018). https://doi.org/10.22630/isim.2018.7.1.2

7. Douloudis, K., Siapera, M., Dimitriou, G., Prentza, A.: Application of automated trust verification and delegation mechanisms in PEPPOL eProcurement network. In: Themistocleous, M., Papadaki, M. (eds.) EMCIS 2019. LNBIP, vol. 381, pp. 448–457. Springer, Cham (2020). https://doi.org/10.1007/978-3-030-44322-1_33

8. Eriksson, H.E., Penker, M.: Business modeling with UML. OMG. Wiley, Nashville (2000)

9. Gao, H., Qin, X., Barroso, R.J.D., Hussain, W., Xu, Y., Yin, Y.: Collaborative learning-based industrial IoT API recommendation for software-defined devices: the implicit knowledge discovery perspective. IEEE Trans. Emerg. Top. Comput. Intell. **6**(1), 66–76 (2022). https://doi.org/10.1109/TETCI.2020.3023155

10. Gunaratne, H., Pappel, I.: Enhancement of the e-invoicing systems by increasing the efficiency of workflows via disruptive technologies. In: Chugunov, A., Khodachek, I., Misnikov, Y., Trutnev, D. (eds.) EGOSE 2020. CCIS, vol. 1349, pp. 60–74. Springer, Cham (2020). https://doi.org/10.1007/978-3-030-67238-6_5

11. Harry Katzan, J., Dowling, W.A.: Software-as-a-service economics. Rev. Bus. Inf. Syst. (RBIS) **14**(1) (2010). https://doi.org/10.19030/rbis.v14i1.500

12. Hernández-Ortega, B.: Key factors for the adoption and subsequent use of e-invoicing. Academia (50), 15 (2012). https://login.wwwproxy1.library.unsw.edu.au/login?url=https://www.proquest.com/scholarly-journals/key-factors-adoption-subsequent-use-e-invoicing/docview/1271600028/se-2?accountid=12763.   Copyright - Copyright Consejo Latinoamericano de Escuelas de Administracion, CLADEA 2012. Accessed 09 Nov 2021; SubjectsTermNotLitGenreText - Spain

13. Koch, B., Billentis: the e-invoicing journey 2019–2025 (2019)

14. Lian, S., Tang, M.: API recommendation for mashup creation based on neural graph collaborative filtering. Connect. Sci. **34**(1), 124–138 (2022). https://doi.org/10.1080/09540091.2021.1974819

15. Marcinkowski, B., Kuciapski, M.: A business process modeling notation extension for risk handling. In: Cortesi, A., Chaki, N., Saeed, K., Wierzchoń, S. (eds.) CISIM 2012. LNCS, vol. 7564, pp. 374–381. Springer, Heidelberg (2012). https://doi.org/10.1007/978-3-642-33260-9_32

16. Marinagi, C., Trivellas, P., Reklitis, P., Skourlas, C.: Drivers and barriers to e-invoicing adoption in Greek large scale manufacturing industries. In: AIP Conference Proceedings, vol. 1644, no. 1 (2015). https://doi.org/10.1063/1.4907852, https://www.osti.gov/biblio/22390959

17. Oyekola, O., Xu, L.: Selecting SaaS CRM solution for SMEs. In: Proceedings of the 10th International Conference on Information Systems and Technologies, ICIST 2020. Association for Computing Machinery, New York (2020). https://doi.org/10.1145/3447568.3448536
18. Papazoglou, M.P., Georgakopoulos, D.: Service-Oriented Computing. MIT Press, Cambridge (2008)
19. Patil, S., Newcomer, E.: ebXML and web services. IEEE Internet Comput. **7**(3), 74–82 (2003). https://doi.org/10.1109/MIC.2003.1200304
20. Peixoto, D., et al.: A comparison of BPMN and UML 2.0 activity diagrams (2008)
21. Qi, L., Song, H., Zhang, X., Srivastava, G., Xu, X., Yu, S.: Compatibility-aware web API recommendation for mashup creation via textual description mining. ACM Trans. Multimedia Comput. Commun. Appl. **17**(1s) (2021). https://doi.org/10.1145/3417293
22. Robbes, R., Lungu, M., Janes, A.: API fluency. In: 2019 IEEE/ACM 41st International Conference on Software Engineering: New Ideas and Emerging Results (ICSE-NIER), pp. 97–100 (2019). https://doi.org/10.1109/ICSE-NIER.2019.00033
23. Wang, X., Liu, X., Liu, J., Chen, X., Wu, H.: A novel knowledge graph embedding based API recommendation method for Mashup development. World Wide Web **24**(3), 869–894 (2021). https://doi.org/10.1007/s11280-021-00894-3
24. Wilde, E., Amundsen, M.: The challenge of API management: API strategies for decentralized API landscapes. In: Companion Proceedings of The 2019 World Wide Web Conference, WWW 2019, pp. 1327–1328. Association for Computing Machinery, New York (2019). https://doi.org/10.1145/3308560.3320089
25. Yuan, W., Nguyen, H.H., Jiang, L., Chen, Y., Zhao, J., Yu, H.: API recommendation for event-driven android application development. Inf. Softw. Technol. **107**, 30–47 (2019). https://doi.org/10.1016/j.infsof.2018.10.010, https://www.sciencedirect.com/science/article/pii/S0950584918302222

Role of Culture in Customer Acceptance of Neobanks

Koen Meijer[✉], Abhishta Abhishta, and Reinoud Joosten

University of Twente, Enschede, The Netherlands
koenmeijerr@gmail.com

Abstract. We examine customer acceptance of neobanks across national cultures using the technology acceptance model (TAM) extended with an additional construct, i.e. trust, accounting for scepticism surrounding digital innovations. We incorporate dimensions developed by Hofstede to evaluate national cultural effects on the modified TAM. For this, we collect primary quantitative data through questionnaires obtaining a sample including many nationalities. We assess our variant of the TAM using partial least squares structural equation modelling to quantify the complex relationships with reflective constructs.

We find that national cultural dimensions may not have a significant effect on the customer acceptance. Moreover, the original two independent constructs of the TAM, *perceived ease of use* and *perceived usefulness*, have a significant positive weak direct effect on acceptance. However, perceived ease of use has a significant positive strong effect on perceived usefulness and *trust*. Finally, the theorised trust dimension has a significant positive weak effect on both the perceived usefulness of, and the *behavioural intention to use* neobanks.

Keywords: Digital Banking · Neobanks · Culture · Digital Transformation

1 Introduction

Technological advancements pave the way for new industries, and change existing industries fundamentally. Indeed, the nature of the financial services industry is being changed by financial technologies, or FinTech, which refers to the use of technology to provide financial solutions [4]. According to KPMG [5], \$60.2B were invested in FinTech companies across 2,914 deals in 2017, \$150.4B across 3,639 deals in 2018, and \$150.4B across 3,286 deals in 2019. Additionally, FinTech start-ups can test technologies and introduce new and innovative products faster than ever before [6]. This allows them to challenge well-established companies.

The concept of FinTech is not novel; it can be traced back to the first financial technology. The Trans-Atlantic transmission cable connecting North America and Europe has been operational since 1866, which provided the foundation for the first period of financial globalisation [4, 7]. This period is called FinTech 1.0, where the financial services industry was interconnected with technology, yet remaining mainly an analogue industry [4, 7].

J. van Hillegersberg et al. (Eds.): FinanceCom 2022, LNBIP 467, pp. 97–116, 2023.
https://doi.org/10.1007/978-3-031-31671-5_7

FinTech 2.0 started at least by 1987 and digitalised the financial services industry [8]. Yet, until 2008, the traditional regulated financial services industry largely controlled developments. Following the financial crisis of 2008 however, the regulatory, operating, and compliance environment changed, facilitating additional rapid advancements [8]. Start-ups and technology companies were beginning to disrupt the traditional industry by delivering their own products and services to business and consumers (e.g. Google Pay, PayPal, and Kickstarter) [6, 8]. This period is dubbed FinTech 3.0 [7].

In recent years a surge of neobanks—independent digital-only entities—in the banking sector occured [9]. They either have a banking licence or partner with traditional banks to deliver their products and services. Typically, neobanks focus on offering newer technologies at lower costs [10], and they can launch features and develop partnerships faster than traditional ones can [11]. To compete with neobanks, traditional banks are launching so called digital banks [9, 12].

By 2020, over 250 neobanks served over 350 million customers [10], inducing fierce competition in customer acquisition and retention in the banking sector [13], so knowledge about customer acceptance is essential to the entire industry. Between countries a remarkable difference in the proportion of consumers banking with neobanks exists, varying between 93 per cent in China for example, and around 4 per cent in the Netherlands and Germany [10]. This begs the question of whether customer acceptance is affected by national cultures.

1.1 Customer Acceptance and Culture

The TAM is predominantly used to measure the customer acceptance of a specific technology. The original model consists of the perceived ease of use of an application, positively impacting its perceived usefulness. Both the perceived ease of use and perceived usefulness constructs are theorized to directly positively affect behavioral intentions to use a technology having a positive impact on the actual system use.

A wide array of studies demonstrate the validity of the TAM, resulting in many revisions of the original version [14–16]. However, only a few have examined effects of national cultural differences on either the original or one of the revised TAMs. An often-used model for comparing national cultural differences is Hofstede's 6-D model. Hofstede [17] distinguished the following four dimensions: power distance, individualism, masculinity, and uncertainty avoidance. Two additional dimensions were added to the model later, namely long- versus short-term orientation, and indulgence [18].

So, two motivational factors for examining the cultural differences exist, namely: (1) the effect that national cultures have on the customer acceptance of neobanks, and (2) how to integrate them into a TAM.

2 Conceptual Model and Hypotheses

We note and address a lack of literature on the customer acceptance of neobanks, presumably since neobanks are a fairly new phenomenon. Also, few studies have incorporated the effects of national cultures in the TAM. Therefore, we examine the influence of national cultures on the TAM applied to neobanks, and insights obtained can be used by neobanks and other ones alike to make crucial strategic decisions. For instance, when expanding to new markets, they can determine where they have a strategic advantage.

Davis [31] devised the original TAM as an adaptation of the theory of reasoned action to tailor to the modelling of user acceptance of information technology. Many studies have shown the validity and reliability of this model [32]. Therefore, our conceptual framework is based on the TAM. On top of the TAM, we take trust into consideration as we found the lack of trust to be a disadvantage for neobanks in our systematic literature review. We add Hofstede's [2] national cultural dimensions to the TAM to measure for possible interaction effects. Our conceptual framework is visualised in Fig. 1.

Davis & Venkatesh [15] mention that research in TAM and psychology suggest that the users' intention to use, is the best predictor of actual system use. Therefore, the behavioural intention to use (BI), is the dependent variable in our study. BI is found to be determined by perceived usefulness (PU), and perceived ease of use (PEOU) [15]. More advanced models have been proposed, heavily catered to a work environment to remove potential biases [31]. We therefore, use the original three constructs.

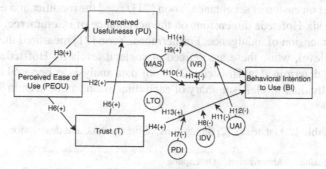

Fig. 1. Conceptual framework

PU is defined as: "the extent to which a person believes that using a particular system would enhance his or her job performance" [3, 15, 31, 33]. Whereas the definition is focussed on job performance, Pikkarainen *et al.* [19] have decided to omit the job aspect, so it can be used as user acceptance outside of the work environment. It is believed that PU is a major determining factor in the acceptance of information technology. Therefore, we formulate Hypothesis 1: *Hypothesis 1. PU has a positive effect on BI.* PEOU, is defined as "the user's perception of the extent to which using a particular system will be free of effort" [3, 15, 31, 33]. Davis [3] mentions that effort is a finite resource, and finds that PEOU has a positive effect on BI. Additionally, PEOU was found to have a positive effect on PU [3]. Therefore, the following two hypotheses are formulated in accordance with the original TAM: *Hypothesis 2. PEOU has a positive effect on BI; Hypothesis 3. PEOU has a positive effect on PU.*

In our systematic literature review, we found that trust is a disadvantage of neobanks compared to traditional banks. Therefore, we look to incorporate trust into the TAM to find potential correlations. Gefen *et al.* [20] modified the existing TAM to incorporate trust for measuring customer acceptance in online shopping. Gefen *et al.* [20] compile a list of previous conceptualisations in the following four options. (1) "a set of specific

beliefs dealing primarily with the integrity, benevolence, and ability of another party",
(2) a general belief that another party can be trusted, sometimes also called trusting
intentions or the 'willingness' of a party to be vulnerable to the actions of another, (3)
affect reflected in feelings of confidence and security in the caring response of the other
party, or (4) a combination of these elements.

According to Gefen *et al.* [20], trust (T) helps a customer reduce social complexity,
which in turn helps reduce subjective undesirable yet possible behaviours. Hence, we
expect T to affect BI positively (cf., Hypothesis 4). Additionally, Gefen *et al.* [20]
mention that using information technology that cannot be trusted will reduce usefulness
(cf., Hypothesis 5). Finally, these authors mention that an unnecessarily hard-to-use
website in the context of eCommerce does not show a consumer that the business cares
or has the ability to care, or even raise suspicion that it is hiding something. Therefore,
we expect PEOU to have a positive effect on T (cf., Hypothesis 6). *Hypothesis 4. T has a
positive effect on BI; Hypothesis 5. T has a positive effect on PU; Hypothesis 6. PEOU
has a positive effect on T.*

We employ Hofstede's [2] national cultural dimensions to measure the national
cultural impact on customer acceptance. Yoon [21] tested the modification effects of five
of the current six Hofstede dimensions on the acceptance of eCommerce. In our study
we add the dimension of indulgence. Furthermore, Yoon [21] measured the dimensions
at a personal level, while these are defined at societal levels by Hofstede [2]. So, we
use the values determined by Hofstede [2] in our data analysis as opposed to measuring
them at an individual level. A summary of each dimension can be seen in Table 1.

Table 1. Hofstede's [2] dimensions, abbreviations, and descriptions.

Hofstede's dimension	Abbreviation	Description
Power distance	PDI	"The extent to which the less powerful members of organizations and institutions accept and expect that power is distributed unequally" [2]
Individualism	IDV	"The degree to which people in a society are integrated into groups" [2]
Masculinity	MAS	"Refers to the distribution of values between the genders which is another fundamental issue for any society" [2]
Uncertainty avoidance	UAI	"The extent to which a culture programs its members to feel either uncomfortable or comfortable in unstructured situations" [2]
Long-term orientation	LTO	"Values found at this pole [long-term] were perseverance, thrift, ordering relationships by status, and having a sense of shame; values at the opposite, short term pole were reciprocating social obligations, respect for tradition, protecting one's 'face', and personal steadiness" [2]
Indulgence	IVR	"Indulgence stands for a society that allows relatively free gratification of basic and natural human desires related to enjoying life and having fun. Restraint stands for a society that controls gratification of needs and regulates it by means of strict social norms" [2]

According to Hofstede [2], most societies are unequal, however some are more unequal than others. Yoon [21] mentions that customers from high PDI countries believe that companies are more likely to take part in unethical behaviour compared to customers from low PDI countries. Thus, we expect customers from high PDI countries to have less trust in neobanks compared to those from low PDI ones. We propose the following hypothesis: *Hypothesis 7. A higher PDI has a negative effect on the relationship between T and BI.* Secondly, IDV measures the degree to which people within a society are integrated into groups [2]. On the one hand, in countries with a low IDV score, individuals are expected to care for themselves, and generally focus more on themselves [2]. According to Yoon [21], individualists identify themselves with a larger society, and they are good at meeting, relying on, and trusting strangers. On the other hand, individuals in a country with a high IDV score, are expected to care and focus on their families or coherent groups [2], and they are unlikely to trust someone outside of their group [21]. Thus, we expect that a higher level of IDV results in a lower effect of T on BI. *Hypothesis 8; A higher IDV has a negative effect on the relationship between T and BI.*

The MAS dimension touches on the distribution of values between the male and female gender [2]. Genders in feminine societies have minimal emotional and social role differentiation, and both genders are expected to be modest and caring [2]. Women in masculine countries are more assertive and competitive than women in feminine countries, but not as much as men [2]. This means that there is maximum emotional and social role differentiation between the genders [2]. Yoon [21] mentions that PU is closely related to achievements of goals and advancement, and therefore we expect the MAS dimension to have a positive effect on the relationship between PU and BI (cf., Hypothesis 9). Additionally, feminine values are also related to creating a comfortable and balanced (work) environment [2, 21]. Effort free use is also concerned with creating a pleasant experience, and for this reason, we argue that a lower degree of the MAS dimension results in a higher effect of PEOU on BI (cf., Hypothesis 10). *Hypothesis 9. A higher MAS has a positive effect on the relationship between PU and BI; Hypothesis 10. A higher MAS dimension has a negative effect on the relationship between PEOU and BI.*

The UAI measures societal discomfort (comfortability) in unstructured (structured) situations [2]. Hofstede [2] mentions that it is not the same as risk avoidance, and that uncertainty avoiding cultures try to reduce the likelihood of unstructured situations by behavioural codes, laws and rules; countries with weak uncertainty avoidance are more accepting of unstructured situations. According to Yoon [21] however, uncertainty avoidance and risk avoidance may have similar effects on trust. Therefore, we argue that the higher the value of the UAI dimension, the lower the effects of T on BI are (cf., Hypothesis 11). Additionally, Straub *et al.* [33] argue that the effect of PU in a higher UAI culture is weakened compared to one with a lower UAI. Therefore, we formulate Hypothesis 12. *Hypothesis 11. A higher UAI has a negative effect on the relationship between T and BI; Hypothesis 12. A higher UAI has a negative effect on the relationship between PU and BI.*

LTO relates to the degree that society focuses on the future. Countries with a higher score on this dimension tend to encourage saving money and efforts in modern education to prepare for the future [2]. Countries that score low on LTO, thus having a short-term orientation, gravitate towards maintaining traditions and norms while being suspicious of societal change [2]. Yoon [21] argues that long-term oriented societies encourage trust, as the future gains outweigh the short-term untrustworthy actions. Hence, we argue that a higher level of the LTO dimension results in a positive modification effect on the relationship between T and BI. *Hypothesis 13. A higher score on LTO has a positive effect on the relationship between T and BI.*

Finally, Hofstede [2] latest addition to the TAM is the indulgence versus restraint (IVR) dimension. A society with indulgence relates to a society that allows for relatively free gratification of basic and natural human desires linked with having fun and enjoying life [2]. Restraint relates to a society that controls this gratification through social norms [2]. As countries with a lower level on this dimension, thus indulgence, tend to remember positive emotions more likely, we argue that this positively affects the relationship between PEOU and BI. Therefore, we formulated the following hypothesis: *Hypothesis 14. A higher level of the IVR dimension has a negative modification effect on the relationship between PEOU and BI.*

3 Data Collection and Analysis

The theoretical constructs mentioned in the previous section – BI, PU, PEOU, and T – are all operationalized using validated items from prior research. We slightly alter the items to fit the topic, however the main concepts of the items remain. The constructs and the questions can be found in Table 2. All of the questions within all of the constructs, apart from trust, are based on validated items from the original creators of the technology acceptance model – namely Davis & Venkatesh [15], most TAM studies use these questions or slightly altered questions. Additionally, we add the relevant and validated items to the PU and PEOU constructs from the study from Gefen *et al.* [20] that incorporated trust for measuring customer acceptance in online shopping. Their validated items are taken into consideration for this study.

Table 2. Constructs and the relevant survey statements.

Construct	Statement
Behavioural intention to use (BI)	(Davis & Venkatesh [15])
BI1	Assuming I have access to a neobank, I intend to use it
BI2	Given that I have access to the system, I predict that I would use it
BI3	I will frequently use the services provided by a neobank
Perceived usefulness (PU)	(Davis & Venkatesh [15]; Gefen *et al.* [20])
PU1	Using a neobank enables me to utilise banking services more quickly

(continued)

Table 2. (*continued*)

Construct	Statement
PU2	Using a neobank improves my performance of utilizing banking services
PU3	Using a neobank for my banking services increases my productivity
PU4	Using a neobank makes it easier for me to utilise banking services
PU5	I find the neobank to be useful for me to utilise banking services
PU6	Using a neobank helps me to save money
Perceived ease of use (PEOU)	(Davis & Venkatesh [15]; Gefen *et al.* [20])
PEOU1	Learning to use the services by a neobank is easy for me
PEOU2	My interaction with the neobank is clear and understandable
PEOU3	I find a neobank to be flexible to interact with
PEOU4	It would be easy for me to become skilful at using the services of a neobank
PEOU5	I find the services of a neobank easy to use
Trust (T)	(Gefen *et al.* [20])
T1	Based on my experience with the neobank in the past, I know it is honest
T2	Based on my experience with the neobank in the past, I know it cares about customers
T3	Based on my experience with the neobank in the past, I know it is not opportunistic
T4	Based on my experience with the neobank in the past, I know it is predictable
T5	Based on my experience with the neobank in the past, I know it is trustworthy

Hinkin [34] finds that reverse scoring items reduce the validity of questionnaire response, and could lead to systematic errors to a scale. Additionally, reverse-scored items are typically employed by researchers to weaken pattern bias, however, item loadings for reverse-scored items were found to be lower than positively worded items that loaded on the same factor [34]. So, we designed our survey in a way that it does not reverse-score items. Furthermore, Hinkin [34] finds that the coefficient alpha reliability with Likert-type scales increase up to the use of five points, and then it levels off. Hence, we designed our survey with a 5-point Likert-type scale.

3.1 Sample Selection

We collected data in our study in two ways – namely by using an online service called Amazon Mechanical Turk, and by spreading the questionnaire on social media. The reason for using the crowdsourcing platform Amazon Mechanical Turk is to have a larger distribution of nationalities in our sample for the measurement of the cultural aspect. Additionally, the gathering of data on social media will be used to achieve data triangulation.

The Amazon Mechanical Turk "workers" have received a reimbursement of €0.5 for filling in the survey. Additionally, for every entry from social media €1,- has been donated to charity. The chosen charity is ShareTheMeal, from the United Nations' World Food Programme. This charity allows a child to be fed for a day for €0.8 and offers complete transparency as to where the meals are distributed. In total, €105,- were donated, equaling 150 meals for children.

The original dataset had a sample size of n = 273, two cases were dropped because of missing Hofstede dimension values. Out of the 271 respondents, 105 came through organic sources (e.g., LinkedIn, WhatsApp, Reddit) whereas the other 166 came through the Amazon Mechanical Turk paid source.

The distribution of the respondents' gender is not entirely balanced (see Table 3), with 200 male respondents, and 69 female respondents, two other cases identified as "other". The gender distribution should theoretically not impact the research, as we do not account for individualistic characteristics in our analysis.

The average age of the participants was 30.04 years old, with a median age of 29. Furthermore, the standard deviation of age is 8.173 years. The age within the sample ranges from 17 to 71, thus having a range of 54 years.

We removed two cases from the analysis due to missing Hofstede values, one from Costa Rica and the other from The Federated States of Micronesia. The major contributors are India with 94 respondents (34.7%), the United States of America with 63 respondents (23.2%), the United Kingdom with 62 respondents (22.9%), and the Netherlands with 17 respondents (6.3%). With the other nationalities having fewer than ten respondents.

Table 3. Descriptive statistics of respondents' characteristics.

Measure	Value	Frequency	Percent
Gender	Male	200	73.8
	Female	69	25.5
	Other	2	0.7
Age	25 or below	93	34.3
	Above 25	178	65.7
Previously used a neobank	Yes	240	88.6
	No	31	11.4

The distribution of the Hofstede dimensions is depicted in Table 4. Each of the Hofstede dimensions ranges on a 0–100 scale. We distribute the dimensions into three categories (low, medium, and high) for descriptive purposes. As can be seen, most of the dimensions tend to have the majority of cases in the medium category. Furthermore, the respondents' values of PDI, IDV, and UAI have more cases in the high category than the low category. For the LTO and IVR dimensions this is the opposite, as they have more cases in the low category compared to the high category. The MAS dimension leftover cases from the medium category are relatively evenly spread over the low and high categories.

Out of the 271 respondents, 240 indicated that they had previously used a neobank (cf., Table 1). The others were considered in our research, as these consumers' perceptions of neobanks still matter for their overall customer acceptance.

3.2 Data Analysis

We analyse the data using using partial least squares path modelling (PLS-SEM) in SmartPLS. This program has the ability to calculate interaction effects in various ways, namely the product-indicator, the two-stage, and the orthogonalisation approach. Henseler et al. [35] mention that a two-stage approach should be employed. According to Fassott et al. [36], in the first stage, the PLS path model is run to obtain the construct scores. These construct scores are then extracted. In the second stage, the interaction term is created by multiplying the construct scores. This interaction term is then inserted as an independent variable and used in a multiple regression on the construct scores of the dependent variable [36]. SmartPLS does all of this automatically.

Following the regression analysis, we analyse the goodness of model fit for both the measurement and structural model. Furthermore, the constructs are operationalised as reflective measurement models, as the reflective measurement model assumes that the covariance among the indicators can be explained by the reflective variable, as opposed to that the indicators build a construct together. We assess these reflective measurement models on construct reliability, convergent validity, discriminant validity, and indicator reliability. Lastly, we test the hypotheses by looking at the path coefficients, the indirect effects, the effect sizes, and the coefficients of determination.

Table 4. Distribution of Hofstede's [2] dimensions in three categories.

Dimension	Low (0 ≤ 30)	Medium(>30–70<)	High (≥70–100)
PDI	1	172	98
IDV	4	112	155
MAS	17	244	10
UAI	0	241	30
LTO	66	198	7
IVR	104	165	2

The first thing to assess before examining the measurement and structural model is the goodness of fit, which measures how well a statistical model fits a set of observations. Two types of models must be examined, namely the saturated model and the estimated model. According to Benitez *et al.* [38], the saturated model allows all of the constructs to be freely correlated, whereas the estimated model is the model specified by the researcher. Three discrepancy measures can be considered and analysed to promote transparency [35]. The three discrepancy measures are the following: the standardised root mean squared residual (SRMR), the unweighted least squares discrepancy (d_{uls}), and the geodesic discrepancy (d_g) [37].

The SRMR was introduced by Henseler *et al.* [39] as a measure for approximate model fit. A value of 0 would indicate a perfect model fit. According to Henseler [35] the SRMR value should be below the threshold of 0.08. This is based on the recommendations by Hu and Bentler [40]. They also mention a 0.10 threshold when being more conservative. The equation for SRMR as stated by Hu & Bentler [40] can be seen in Eq. 1, where; p = number of observed variables, s_{ij} = observed covariances, $\hat{o}_{ij}$ = the reproduced covariances, s_{ii} and s_{jj} are the observed standard deviations.

$$\text{SRMR} = \sqrt{\left\{2\sum_{i=1}^{p}\sum_{j=1}^{i}\left[\left(s_{ij} - \hat{o}_{ij}\right)/\left(s_{ii}s_{jj}\right)\right]^2\right\} \div p(p+1)} \tag{1}$$

Limited information is available surrounding the usefulness, behaviour, relevance, and application of exact model fit criteria. We use bootstrap confidence interval results to estimate the exact model fits, and these are recommended to be below the 95% or 99% quantile [37]. This method can be applied to the bootstrap confidence interval of SRMR, however also of the d_{uls} and d_g [41]. d_{uls} and d_g are two approaches to quantify how much the empirical correlation matrix differs from the model-implied correlation matrix [35]. We interpret these values against the confidence intervals, as these values cannot be interpreted on their own [37]. Klesel *et al.* [42] mention the distance functions depicted in Eq. 2 and Eq. 3, where; K = number of rows from each correlation matrix, $\sigma_{ij,1}$ and $\sigma_{ij,2}$ are elements of the respective correlation matrices, and φ_i = the i-th eigenvalue of the correlation matrix.

$$d_{uls} = \tfrac{1}{2}\sum_{i=1}^{K}\left(\sigma_{ij,1} - \sigma_{ij,2}\right)^2 \tag{2}$$

$$d_g = \tfrac{1}{2}\sum_{i=1}^{K}\ln(\varphi_i)^2 \tag{3}$$

The saturated and estimated model fits prior to the removal of indicators are shown in Table 5. The model fit greatly improved after removing the indicators, which can be seen in Table 6. The SRMR was initially above the 0.08 threshold for both the models, but below the more lenient 0.10 threshold. After removing some indicators, the SRMR was 0.07 for the saturated model, well below the recommended threshold, and 0.082 for the estimated model, slightly above the 0.08 threshold but well below the 0.10 threshold. Thus, the SRMR indicates a relatively good model fit. When using bootstrapped confidence intervals to determine the exact model fit, all values are outside the 99% confidence interval, thus indicating a bad model fit. We also attempted to remove non-neobank users from the analysis, however this did not improve the approximate nor exact model fit. Sarstedt *et al.* [43] mention that researchers should be cautious when reporting and using model fit in PLS-SEM, as the criteria are in the early stages of research. For this reason, we decided to continue with our research despite not meeting the exact model fit criteria.

Table 5. Saturated and estimated model fit prior to the removal of indicators.

	Goodness of Model Fit (Saturated Model)			Goodness of Model Fit (Estimated Model)		
	Value	HI95	HI99	Value	HI95	HI99
SRMR	0.086	0.052	0.055	0.099	0.059	0.061
d_{uls}	2.390	0.082	0.970	3.173	1.123	1.216
d_g	0.579	0.351	0.375	0.647	0.386	0.423

Table 6. Saturated and estimated model fit after the removal of indicators.

	Goodness of Model Fit (Saturated Model)			Goodness of Model Fit (Estimated Model)		
	Value	HI95	HI99	Value	HI95	HI99
SRMR	0.070	0.048	0.050	0.082	0.056	0.060
d_{uls}	1.024	0.481	0.527	1.422	0.648	0.754
d_g	0.395	0.253	0.273	0.452	0.288	0.324

SmartPLS allows for the assessment of construct reliability, or composite reliability, through various measures—Cronbach's Alpha, Dijkstra-Henseler's rho (ρ_A), and composite reliability. These values range between 0 and 1, and a higher value indicates better reliability. According to Benitez *et al.* [38], Dijkstra-Henseler's ρ_A should be used. Dijkstra & Henseler [44] denote the equation for ρ_A as seen in Eq. 4, where; $\widehat{w}$ = the estimated weight vector of the latent variable, $\widehat{w}'$ = the number of indicators directly associated with the latent variable in $\widehat{w}$, and S = the empirical covariance matrix of the respective indicator.

$$\rho_A = \left(\widehat{w}'\widehat{w}\right)^2 * \frac{\widehat{w}'(S-diag(S))\widehat{w}'}{\widehat{w}'\left(\widehat{w}\widehat{w}'-diag\left(\widehat{w}\widehat{w}'\right)\right)\widehat{w}} \tag{4}$$

A value greater than 0.707 is desirable as this indicates that the latent variable can explain over 50% of the variance in the construct scores. The values for ρ_A can be found in Table 7 before the removal of the indicators. In both instances, all the values are above 0.707. The other two measures were also taken into consideration and show identical results. These values indicate reliable constructs.

Convergent validity measures the degree to which indicators that measure the same construct are related, and the average variance extracted (AVE) is typically used to

Table 7. Evaluation of the reflective measurement models.

Code	Construct/Indicator	ρ_A	AVE	Weight	Loading
	Behavioural intention to use (BI) (1: strongly disagree, 5: strongly agree) (Composite measurement model, mode B, dominant indicator: BI1)	0.765	0.671		
BI1	Assuming I have access to a neobank, I intend to use it			0.455***	0.863***
BI2	Given that I have access to the system, I predict that I would use it			0.402***	0.798***
BI3	I will frequently use the services provided by a neobank			0.361***	0.794***
	Perceived usefulness (PU) (1: strongly disagree, 5: strongly agree) (Composite measurement model, mode B, dominant indicator: PU1)	0.794	0.465		
PU1	Using a neobank enables me to utilise banking services more quickly			0.304***	0.761***
PU2	Using a neobank improves my performance of utilizing banking services			0.281***	0.755***
PU3	Using a neobank for my banking services increases my productivity			0.180***	0.633***
PU4	Using a neobank makes it easier for me to utilise banking services			0.241***	0.710***
PU5	I find the neobank to be useful for me to utilise banking services			0.281***	0.731***
PU6	Using a neobank helps me to save money			0.149***	0.451***
	Perceived ease of use (PEOU): (1: strongly disagree, 5: strongly agree) (Composite measurement model, mode B, dominant indicator: PEOU1)	0.803	0.558		
PEOU1	Learning to use the services by a neobank is easy for me			0.270***	0.750***
PEOU2	My interaction with the neobank is clear and understandable			0.276***	0.766***
PEOU3	I find a neobank to be flexible to interact with			0.254***	0.683***
PEOU4	It would be easy for me to become skilful at using the services of a neobank			0.265***	0.756***

(continued)

Table 7. (*continued*)

Code	Construct/Indicator	ρ_A	AVE	Weight	Loading
PEOU5	I find the services of a neobank easy to use			0.273***	0.778***
	Trust (T): (1: strongly disagree, 5: strongly agree) (Composite measurement model, mode B, dominant indicator: T1)	0.874	0.591		
T1	Based on my experience with the neobank in the past, I know it is honest			0.354***	0.824***
T2	Based on my experience with the neobank in the past, I know it cares about customers			0.292***	0.802***
T3	Based on my experience with the neobank in the past, I know it is not opportunistic			0.159***	0.708***
T4	Based on my experience with the neobank in the past, I know it is predictable			0.154***	0.662***
T5	Based on my experience with the neobank in the past, I know it is trustworthy			0.312***	0.832***

Note: * p < 0.05, ** p < 0.01, *** p < 0.001 (lower p-values indicate greater confidence of the statistical test), one-tailed t-test (df = 239)

measure it [38]. The AVE shows how much of the variance in the indicators is explained by the latent variable [38]. A value of 0.5 is suggested by Benitez *et al.* [38] as this means that the latent variable can explain 50% of the variance in an indicator. Henseler *et al.* [45] state the formula seen in Eq. 5, where; ξ_j = the construct, λ_{jk} = the indicator loading, K_j = the number of indicators of the construct, and Θ_{jk} = the error variance of the kth indicator. The values from BI, PEOU, and T are above the 0.5 mark, but PU is below it before removing several indicators. After the removal of several indicators, all values are above the 0.5 mark, indicating good convergent validity.

$$AVE\xi_j = \frac{\sum_{k=1}^{K_j} \lambda_{jk}^2}{\sum_{k=1}^{K_j} \lambda_{jk}^2 + \Theta_{jk}} \quad (5)$$

Discriminant validity measures whether or not reflective variables are different enough to represent two theoretical concepts [38]. Benitez *et al.* [38] and Henseler *et al.* [45] mention that the heterotrait-monotrait ratio (HTMT) should be used to assess discriminant validity. Henseler *et al.* [45] state Eq. 6, where; ξ_j and ξ_i are two different constructs, and K_j and K_i are their indicators.

$$HTMT_{ij} = \frac{1}{K_i K_j} \sum_{g=1}^{K_i} \sum_{h=1}^{K_j} r_{ig,jh} \div \left(\frac{2}{K_i(K_i-1)} * \sum_{g=1}^{K_i} \sum_{h=1}^{K_j} r_{ig,ih} * \frac{2}{K_j(K_j-1)} * \sum_{g=1}^{K_i} \sum_{h=1}^{K_j} r_{jg,jh} \right) \quad (6)$$

The value should be below 0.85 or 0.90, where the 0.85 mark is the stricter one [39, 45]. The HTMT values before the removal of indicators can be found in Table 8. Note that only PEOU and BI exceed the 0.9 mark. PU and BI, and PU and PEOU have a value greater than 0.85. The three previous values are now above 0.9. Additionally, one can look at the bootstrapped values, these should be and are lower than 1 [37]. The values above 0.9 can be taken with a grain of salt because discriminant validity is only relevant to constructs that are similar, which is not the case for the constructs violating the HTMT criteria—BI and PU, BI and PEOU, PU and PEOU.

Table 8. Heterotrait-monotrait ratio prior to the removal of indicators.

	BI	PU	PEOU
BI	-	-	-
PU	0.855	-	-
PEOU	0.906	0.879	-
T	0.511	0.663	0.623

Finally, indicator reliability should be examined. According to Hair *et al.* [46] indicator reliability is the degree to which a set of indicators are internally consistent with their measurements. Benitez [38] mention that the unsquared factor loadings should be above 0.707, and the squared factor loadings above 0.499. The unsquared factor loadings can be seen in Table 7.

Initially, we found PU3, PU6, PEOU3, and T4 below the recommended threshold. Additionally, after removing T4, T3 had a value below 0.707, and was therefore removed. We removed the indicators following a stepwise approach by starting at the lowest loadings, as the loadings are recalculated after each removal. The removal of the indicators vastly improved the model fit, the AVE, and the construct reliability. However, it slightly worsened the discriminant validity as mentioned before. Furthermore, in both instances the factors were found to be significant at 0.001.

In Sect. 3, fourteen hypotheses were formulated, to be tested in accordance with the path coefficients and the confidence intervals. Path coefficients are standardised regression coefficients. The path coefficients indicate the change in standard deviations of the dependent variable when an independent variable increases by one standard deviation while keeping all other constructs unchanged [35, 38]. One can look at the t-values to determine the significance, however one can also look at the 95% confidence interval. When this does not cross the zero mark, there is at least a significant effect at a p-value of 0.05 [38] (Table 9).

Besides the path coefficients, the effect sizes are also shown in Table 6. Cohen's [47] f^2 equal or greater than 0.35 indicates a strong effect, equal or greater than 0.15 and less than 0.35 a moderate effect, equal or greater than 0.02 and less than 0.15 a weak effect, and less than 0.02 an unsubstantial effect [36].

As can be seen in Table 7, H1, H2, H3, H5, and H6 are significant at a p-value of 0.001, whereas H4 is significant at an alpha level of 0.01. The path coefficient for PU on BI is 0.321, meaning that BI moves 0.321 standard deviations when PU moves one standard deviation. Furthermore, it has a weak effect size ($f^2 = 0.103$). PEOU on BI has a path coefficient of 0.329 and has a weak effect size ($f^2 = 0.097$). PEOU on perceived

Table 9. Path coefficients and effect sizes.

Relationship	Path coefficients	Cohen's f^2
H1 I PU --> BI	0.321*** (4.505) [0.199, 0.435]	0.103
H2 I PEOU --> BI	0.329*** (4.194) [0.194, 0.451]	0.097
H3 I PEOU --> PU	0.613*** (12.043) [0.526, 0.693]	0.588
H4 I T --> BI	0.171** (2.632) [0.071, 0.288]	0.037
H5 I T --> PU	0.198*** (3.419) [0.104, 0.292]	0.061
H6 I PEOU --> T	0.537*** (11.992) [0.469, 0.612]	0.406
H7 I PDI * T --> BI	−0.157 (1.021) [−0.360, 0.131]	0.014
H8 I IDV * T --> BI	−0.240 (1.445) [−0.484, 0.042]	0.026
H9 I MAS * PU --> BI	−0.050 (0.588) [−0.146, 0.122]	0.005
H10 I MAS * PEOU --> BI	0.012 (0.132) [−0.152, 0.140]	0.000
H11 I UAI * T --> BI	−0.056 (0.989) [−0.139, 0.040]	0.005
H12 I UAI * PU --> BI	0.043 (0.771) [−0.040, 0.138]	0.004
H13 I LTO * T --> BI	−0.036 (0.595) [−0.128, 0.069]	0.003
H14 I IVR * PEOU --> BI	−0.055 (0.860) [−0.149, 0.064]	0.004

Note: * p < 0.05, ** p < 0.01, *** p < 0.001 (lower p-values indicate greater confidence of the statistical test), one tailed t-values in parentheses, 95% bootstrap percentile confidence intervals in brackets.

usefulness PU has a path coefficient of 0.613 and a strong effect size ($f^2 = 0.588$). The path coefficient of T on BI is 0.171 and has a weak effect size ($f^2 = 0.037$). Furthermore, T on PU also has a weak effect size ($f^2 = 0.061$). And a path coefficient of 0.198. Lastly, PEOU on T has a path coefficient of 0.537 and a strong effect size ($f^2 = 0.406$). We have enough statistical evidence to reject null hypotheses $H1_0$, $H2_0$, $H3_0$, $H4_0$, $H5_0$, and $H6_0$.

Additionally, all the interaction effects by the Hofstede dimensions are insignificant at a p-value of 0.05. Furthermore, the effect sizes across hypotheses H7 throughout H14 are all unsubstantial. This means that there is not enough statistical evidence to reject the null hypotheses and allows us to assume that the Hofstede dimensions do not have an interaction effect on either of the independent variables (PU, PEOU, and T) on behavioural intention to use (BI).

Finally, we inspect the unadjusted and adjusted coefficients of determination. The coefficients of determination indicate how much variance can be explained in a dependent variable by an independent variable [35]. Whereas the unadjusted R^2 does not take the sample size or the number of independent variables into consideration, the adjusted R^2 does [39]. The latter is most often used in more complex models and will always be lower. Both coefficients of determination will be denoted, however as this model is complex, the adjusted R^2 should be considered. The unadjusted R^2 of BI is 0.647, and the adjusted R^2 is 0.623. This means that either 64.7% or 62.3% of the variance in BI can be explained by PU, PEOU, and T. Furthermore, the unadjusted and adjusted R^2 of

PU is respectively 0.545 and 0.542, which means that 54.5% or 54.2% can be explained by the independent variables PEOU and T. Lastly, the coefficients of determination for T are 0.289 (unadjusted R^2), and 0.286 (adjusted R^2). Therefore, connoting that 28.9% or 28.6% of the variance can be explained by PEOU.

4   Conclusions

Neobanks are still in the early stages of development, and the majority of the customers are innovators or early adopters. The most frequently observed strategy by neobanks is cost leadership through offering competitive prices, lower loan rates, and higher interest rates [28]. Consumers favour these business models, however neobanks require a large customer base for them to be profitable, which is challenging because of the high competition in customer acquisition and retention [13, 23, 27].

We believe it is of utmost importance for neobanks to increase the customers' behavioural intention to use them. One way to improve their customer acceptance is by improving the perceived usefulness of their services and products. Neobanks are not bound to legacy systems, so we recommend them to **use their agility when it comes to operations and technology deployment**, allowing them to adapt quickly to changing customer needs [22, 29]. Finally, neobanks currently offer superior technology over traditional banks, and we suggest that the former **keep investing in technology** to stay ahead of the competition.

Our findings show that the most crucial factor in increasing customer acceptance is for neobanks to focus on improving customers' perceived ease of use, as this aspect showed the most substantial effects. In addition, we found in our literature review that customers—mainly the younger demographic—are frustrated with the outdated user experience offered by incumbents [22, 24, 25, 30]. Therefore, we suggest neobanks continue to **promote clear, understandable, and easy-to-use services** to maintain a competitive advantage and increase the consumers' intention to use them.

Additionally, we found that building trust is more cumbersome for neobanks, because trust is built on personal relationships over time, and digital platforms are perceived to be riskier [1, 25]. As previously mentioned, trust had a positive weak effect on the behavioural intention to use a neobank. To overcome this disadvantage, we advise neobanks to promote trust actively by **having transparent and straightforward user interfaces and interactions with their customers**. An example of how neobanks can promote transparency is by respecting consumers' control over privacy by being transparent in the collection and use of consumer data [25]. As neobanks are in the relatively early stages, we believe that time is needed for the majority of consumers to become acquainted and comfortable with them. After all, early adopters are dissimilar in the risk propensity compared to the majority formed by later adopters [48].

Finally, an important part of our investigations was to see whether national cultural differences impact the customer acceptance of neobanks. We found no significant interaction effects between the Hofstede dimensions and the modified TAM. Neobanks can use this information in several ways. Firstly, this indicates that neobanks do not need to change their business model across various countries to be accepted by customers, making expansions into other regions less complicated. Compared to traditional banks, neobanks can more rapidly expand due to their lean business models for which neither physical branches nor additional employees are needed. However, the regulatory framework should also be taken into consideration. Unlicenced neobanks are at an advantage over licensed neobanks, as they partner with incumbents to comply with regulations, which is faster than acquiring a banking licence [25, 26, 28]. However, a disadvantage is that these unlicenced neobanks can only offer a limited number of services and benefits compared to licenced ones, meaning that the services might not always live up to the customers' needs.

5   Limitations and Future Work

Our study has some limitations. First, in our literature review we did not employ a snowballing method, which could have resulted in a broader range of articles. The reason for not utilising this method is because the literature review was not our primary focus and it was performed to aid in the formulation of the method. Overall, the snowballing method would not have led to different results, however it could have resulted in additional insights. Secondly, we did not question the participants in a controlled environment. Additionally, the participants have experiences with different neobanks, which can mean that experiences vary. This means that the results are harder to generalize. An improvement would have been to have all the participants use a determined neobank or a set of neobanks, which would be followed by the designed questionnaire. This might change the perspectives of individuals who have not used neobanks before and might more accurately measure the TAM.

Furthermore, there may be a participation bias because most respondents used a neobank before. This indicates that they are less sceptical of neobanks than those that have not used a neobank before, which could have impacted the results. Finally, in the data analysis, we found that the model fit was suboptimal for the estimated model and the saturated model. Although the model fit criteria are in the early stages of research, and researchers are not certain whether it should be applied on PLS-SEM, this limitation should still be noted. Our study also did not tackle individual characteristics, such as age, which could influence the behavioural intention to use a neobank. We collected basic control variables, however these were not used in the data analysis as this was not the main focus of our study and would have complicated the conceptual model and the data analysis process significantly.

References

1. Tosun, P.: Brand trust for digital-only bank brands: consumer insights from an emerging market. Presented at the ATLAS 7th International Conference on Social Sciences, Budapest, Hungary (2020). http://openaccess.mef.edu.tr/xmlui/handle/20.500.11779/1370. Accessed 04 Dec 2020
2. Hofstede, G.: Dimensionalizing cultures: the Hofstede model in context. Online Read. Psychol. Cult. 2(1), 1–26 (2011). https://doi.org/10.9707/2307-0919.1014
3. Davis, F.D.: Perceived usefulness, perceived ease of use, and user acceptance of information technology. MIS Q. 13(3), 319–340 (1989). https://doi.org/10.2307/249008

4. Arner, D.W., Barberis, J., Buckley, R.P.: The evolution of FinTech: a new post-crisis paradigm. Georget. J. Int. Law **47**, 1271–1319 (2015/2016)
5. Pollari, I., Ruddenklau, A.: Pulse of FinTech H1 2020. KPMG (2020). https://home.kpmg/xx/en/home/industries/financial-services/pulse-of-fintech.html. Accessed 12 Sept 2020
6. Goldstein, I., Jiang, W., Karolyi, G.A.: To FinTech and beyond. Rev. Financ. Stud. **32**(5), 1647–1661 (2019). https://doi.org/10.1093/rfs/hhz025
7. Leong, K., Sung, A.: FinTech (financial technology): what is it and how to use technologies to create business value in FinTech way? Int. J. Innov. Manag. Technol. 74–78 (2018). https://doi.org/10.18178/ijimt.2018.9.2.791
8. Arner, D.W., Barberis, J., Buckley, R.P.: FinTech, RegTech, and the reconceptualization of financial regulation. Northwest. J. Int. Law Bus. **37**(3), 373–415 (2017)
9. Stuart, R.: Neobank or digital bank or bricks and mortar bank? Fullstack (2019). https://www.fullstack.com.au/neobank-or-digital-bank-or-bricks-and-mortar-bank/. Accessed 15 Sept 2020
10. Revolut. https://www.revolut.com. Accessed 05 Oct 2020
11. Dobson, A.: What are neobanks and how are they changing financial services? PA Consulting. https://www.paconsulting.com/insights/what-are-neobanks-and-how-are-they-changing-financial-services/. Accessed 15 Sept 2020
12. Minarchenko, I.M., Saiko, I.L.: The future of neobanks in the development of banking sector. UDC **336**, 335–337 (2018)
13. Lee, I., Shin, Y.J.: FinTech: ecosystem, business models, investment decisions, and challenges. Bus. Horiz. **61**(1), 35–46 (2018). https://doi.org/10.1016/j.bushor.2017.-09.003
14. Venkatesh, V., Davis, F.D.: A theoretical extension of the technology acceptance model: four longitudinal field studies. Manag. Sci. **46**(2), 186–204 (2000). https://doi.org/10.1287/mnsc.46.2.186.11926
15. Davis, F.D., Venkatesh, V.: A critical assessment of potential measurement biases in the technology acceptance model: three experiments. Int. J. Hum. Comput. Stud. **45**(1), 19–45 (1996). https://doi.org/10.1006/ijhc.1996.0040
16. Adams, D.A., Nelson, R.R., Todd, P.A.: Perceived usefulness, ease of use, and usage of information technology: a replication. MIS Q. **16**(2), 227–247 (1992). https://doi.org/10.2307/249577
17. Hofstede, G.: National cultures in four dimensions: a research-based theory of cultural differences among nations. Int. Stud. Manag. Organ. **13**(1–2), 46–74 (1983). https://doi.org/10.1080/00208825.1983.11656358
18. The 6D model of national culture. Geert Hofstede (2016). https://geerthofstede.com/culture-geert-hofstede-gert-jan-hofstede/6d-model-of-national-culture/. Accessed 15 Sept 2020
19. Pikkarainen, T., Pikkarainen, K., Karjaluoto, H., Pahnila, S.: Consumer acceptance of online banking: an extension of the technology acceptance model. Internet Res. **14**(3), 224–235 (2004). https://doi.org/10.1108/10662240410542652
20. Gefen, D., Karahanna, E., Straub, D.W.: Trust and TAM in online shopping: an integrated model. MIS Q. **27**(1), 51–90 (2003). https://doi.org/10.2307/30036519
21. Yoon, C.: The effects of national culture values on consumer acceptance of e-commerce: online shoppers in China. Inf. Manag. **46**(5), 294–301 (2009). https://doi.org/10.1016/j.im.2009.06.001
22. Vives, X.: Digital disruption in banking. Annu. Rev. Financ. Econ. **11**(1), 243–272 (2019). https://doi.org/10.1146/annurev-financial-100719-120854
23. Wewege, L., Lee, J., Thomsett, M.: Disruptions and digital banking trends. J. Appl. Finance Bank. **10**(6), 15–56 (2020)
24. Tardieu, H., Daly, D., Esteban-Lauzán, J., Hall, J., Miller, G.: Case study 7: the digital transformation of banking—an industry changing beyond recognition. In: Tardieu, H., Daly, D.,

Esteban-Lauzán, J., Hall, J., Miller, G. (eds.) Deliberately Digital: Rewriting Enterprise DNA for Enduring Success, pp. 281–292. Springer, Cham (2020). https://doi.org/10.1007/978-3-030-37955-1_28

25. Valero, S., Climent, F., Esteban, R.: Future banking scenarios. Evolution of digitalisation in Spanish banking. J. Bus. Accouting Finance Perspect. **2**(2), Article no. 2 (2020). https://doi.org/10.35995/jbafp2020013

26. Saksonova, S., Kuzmina-Merlino, I.: FinTech as financial innovation – the possibilities and problems of implementation. Eur. Res. Stud. J. **20**(3A), 961–973 (2017)

27. Gouveia, L.B., Perun, M., Daradkeh, Y.I.: Digital transformation and customers services: the banking revolution. Int. J. Open Inf. Technol. **8**(7), 124–128 (2020)

28. Buchi, G., Cugno, M., Fasolo, L., Zerbetto, A., Castagnoli, R.: New banks in the 4th industrial revolution: a review and typology. Thessaloniki, Greece, pp. 74–96 (2019). https://iris.unito.it/handle/2318/1716255#.X8eVPGhKj-g. Accessed 02 Dec 2020

29. Ryan, J.: The new emerging banks and their role in payments. In: The Paytech Book: The Payment Technology Handbook for Investors, Entrepreneurs, and FinTech Visionaries, 1st edn, pp. 28–30. Wiley (2019). https://doi.org/10.1002/9781119551973.ch8

30. Arslanian, H., Fischer, F.: Fintech and the future of the financial ecosystem. In: Arslanian, H., Fischer, F. (eds.) The Future of Finance: the Impact of FinTech, AI, and Crypto on Financial Services, pp. 201–216. Springer, Cham (2019). https://doi.org/10.1007/978-3-030-14533-0_16

31. Davis, F.D., Bagozzi, R.P., Warshaw, P.R.: User acceptance of computer technology: a comparison of two theoretical models. Manag. Sci. **35**(8), 982–1003 (1989). https://doi.org/10.1287/mnsc.35.8.982

32. Lee, Y., Kozar, K.A., Larsen, K.R.T.: The technology acceptance model: past, present, and future. Commun. Assoc. Inf. Syst. **12**, 752–780 (2003). https://doi.org/10.17705/1CAIS.01250

33. Straub, D., Keil, M., Brenner, W.: Testing the technology acceptance model across cultures: a three country study. Inf. Manag. **33**(1), 1–11 (1997). https://doi.org/10.1016/S0378-7206(97)00026-8

34. Hinkin, T.R.: A review of scale development practices in the study of organizations. J. Manag. **21**(5), 967–988 (1995)

35. Henseler, J., Dijkstra, T.K.: ADANCO 2.0.1 user manual. Composite Modeling (2017)

36. Fassott, G., Henseler, J., Coelho, P.S.: Testing moderating effects in PLS path models with composite variables. Ind. Manag. Data Syst. **116**(9), 1887–1900 (2016). https://doi.org/10.1108/IMDS-06-2016-0248

37. Henseler, J., Hubona, G., Ray, P.A.: Using PLS path modeling in new technology research: updated guidelines. Ind. Manag. Data Syst. **116**(1), 2–20 (2015). https://doi.org/10.1108/IMDS-09-2015-0382

38. Benitez, J., Henseler, J., Castillo, A., Schuberth, F.: How to perform and report an impactful analysis using partial least squares: guidelines for confirmatory and explanatory IS research. Inf. Manag. **57**(2), 1–16 (2019). https://doi.org/10.1016/j.im.2019.05.003

39. Henseler, J., et al.: Common beliefs and reality about PLS: comments on Rönkkö and Evermann (2013). Organ. Res. Methods **17**(2), 182–209 (2014). https://doi.org/10.1177/1094428114526928

40. Hu, L., Bentler, P.M.: Cutoff criteria for fit indexes in covariance structure analysis: conventional criteria versus new alternatives. Struct. Equ. Model. **6**(1), 1–55 (1999). https://doi.org/10.1080/10705519909540118

41. Dijkstra, T.K., Henseler, J.: Consistent and asymptotically normal PLS estimators for linear structural equations. Comput. Stat. Data Anal. **81**, 10–23 (2015). https://doi.org/10.1016/j.csda.2014.07.008

42. Klesel, M., Schuberth, F., Henseler, J., Niehaves, B.: A test for multigroup comparison using partial least squares path modeling. Internet Res. **29**(3), 464–477 (2019). https://doi.org/10.1108/IntR-11-2017-0418

43. Sarstedt, M., Ringle, C.M., Hair, J.F.: Partial least squares structural equation modeling. In: Homburg, C., Klarmann, M., Vomberg, A. (eds.) Handbook of Market Research, pp. 1–40. Springer, Cham (2017). https://doi.org/10.1007/978-3-319-05542-8_15-1

44. Dijkstra, T.K., Henseler, J.: Consistent partial least squares path modeling. MIS Q. **39**, 297–316 (2015). https://doi.org/10.25300/MISQ/2015/39.2.02

45. Henseler, J., Ringle, C.M., Sarstedt, M.: A new criterion for assessing discriminant validity in variance-based structural equation modeling. J. Acad. Mark. Sci. **43**(1), 115–135 (2014). https://doi.org/10.1007/s11747-014-0403-8

46. Hair, J.F., Black, W.C., Babin, B.J., Anderson, R.E.: Multivariate Data Analysis, 7th edn. Pearson Education, Harlow (2013)

47. Cohen, J.: Statistical Power Analysis for the Behavioral Sciences, 2nd edn. Lawrence Erlbaum Associates, Hillsdale (1988)

48. Frattini, F., Bianchi, M., De Massis, A., Sikimic, U.: The role of early adopters in the diffusion of new products: differences between platform and nonplatform innovations: early adopters of platform innovations. J. Prod. Innov. Manag. **31**(3), 466–488 (2014). https://doi.org/10.1111/jpim.12108

From Perceived Mobility to the Intention to Use Mobile Payments: The Role of Positive and Negative Determinants

Petar Dzelalija[1] and Ana Ivanisevic Hernaus[2]([✉]) [iD]

[1] Audit Services, KPMG Croatia, 10000 Zagreb, Croatia
[2] Faculty of Economics and Business, University of Zagreb, J. F. Kennedy 6, 10000 Zagreb, Croatia

aivanisev@net.efzg.hr

Abstract. Mobile payments have become an important service and tool for managing personal finance in the digital era. However, there is a dearth of research focused on underlying mechanisms and boundary conditions driving a consumer's decision to use mobile payments for everyday transactions. Therefore, by departing from TAM and TRAM frameworks, we investigated the predictive role of mobile payment antecedents. Both moderating and/or mediating effects were examined through conditional process analyses on the field survey sample of 218 financially educated individuals. We confirmed the mediating role of mobile payment knowledge in the relationship between perceived mobility and intention to use mobile payments, as well as moderating roles of perceived compatibility and perceived risk. Moreover, we were able to validate our comprehensive research model and extend the demographic and regional scope of the related research, going beyond the mainstream findings focused on generation X or Z consumers from emerging and developing markets.

Keywords: Mobile Payments · Perceived Mobility · Intention to Use Mobile Payments · Technology Readiness and Acceptance Model (TAM) · Conditional Process Analysis

1 Introduction

FinTech is reshaping financial industry by leaning towards personalized financial services [1]. Traditional delivery channels (i.e., bank branches and automatic teller machines) have been endangered by innovative digitalized alternatives (i.e., internet and mobile banking). Mobile payments in particular have become an important service and tool for managing personal finance in the digital era [2]. Despite of emerging as a mainstream consumer delivery channel [3], people still perceive the value of the mobile payment services differently. Their attitude towards using mobile communication technology on intelligent devices to make financial transactions determines the intention to use mobile payments (e.g. [4, 5]).

J. van Hillegersberg et al. (Eds.): FinanceCom 2022, LNBIP 467, pp. 117–132, 2023.
https://doi.org/10.1007/978-3-031-31671-5_8

Within the literature, a respectful number of studies [6, 7] have investigated and identified the most common drivers of mobile payment adoption (such as perceived usefulness, perceived ease of use, perceived risk, perceived cost). However, there is still a dearth of research focused on underlying mechanisms and boundary conditions driving a consumer's decision to use mobile payments for everyday transactions.

Therefore, the present study aims to provide insights about whether and under which circumstances the perceived mobility (i.e., "the ability to access services ubiquitously, on the move, and via wireless networks and a variety of mobile devices"; [8] and mobile payment knowledge (i.e., consumer familiarity and experience [expertise] of using mobile payments; [9]) drive the intention to use mobile payment channels in the future. By revising the dominantly-used Technology Acceptance Model – TAM [10] and extending the less-known Technology Readiness and Acceptance Model – TRAM [11], we investigate the predictive role of mobile payment antecedents. Both moderating and/or mediating effects were examined through conditional process analyses (i.e., the mediation, moderation and moderated mediation models, see Fig. 1) conducted using the survey sample of 218 financially educated individuals at the public university (Croatia).

Our study contributes by clarifying theoretical underpinnings of the antecedents (both enablers and inhibitors) of the intention to use mobile payments. We clearly delineated and highlighted the role and causal nature of different constructs of interest. By examining moderation–mediation effects, we not only applied a novel methodological approach to the field (i.e., conditional process analysis; [12]); we likewise offered a deeper understanding of the phenomenon (using TRAM as a baseline) that is currently lacking in the literature (e.g. [13]). Additionally, our data on young consumers' mobile payment behaviors and preferences were obtained and cover the EU member country that has not been previously investigated. Thus, we were able to validate our comprehensive research model and extend the demographic and regional scope of the related research, going beyond the mainstream findings focused on generation X or Z consumers from emerging and developing markets [6].

2 Theory and Hypotheses

2.1 FinTech and Mobile Payments

The global availability of a smartphone, the expansion in the coverage of mobile phone networks and other technological advances driven by the internet revolution changed the face of the financial services industry [14, 15]). Nowadays both banks and non-banking entities offer various FinTech services (including mobile financial services; see [16]) that have attracted a considerable number of consumers worldwide (64% coverage in 2019; [17]). The focus of the present research is on mobile payments (i.e., innovative systems that enable consumers to use banking and other payment services on mobile devices; [7]) as they represent a growing financial market segment [9]. In particular, hereby we address the usage of the entire spectrum of mobile transactions (e.g. mobile banking, mobile money, mobile wallets).

Mobile banking represents a service through which consumers can access their accounts remotely via a mobile device to check balances, transfer funds, pay bills, make investments and perform various other transactions [14, 18]. Mobile money is defined as "a branchless banking model that provides financial services through a mobile device" [19]. It can be operated by means of a mobile wallet, which refers to "a digital repository of electronic money that is implemented via mobile devices" [20].

As an alternative to traditional delivery channel, these types of mobile payments have brought convenience [21] and have the ability to improve consumer satisfaction [16]. Given the increasing use of and demand for mobile payments, a growing body of quantitative field survey studies has been published with an intention to identify complex drivers of adoption [13, 22].

2.2 TAM and TRAM as Theoretical Frameworks to Study the Mobile Payment Adoption

Two-thirds of studies (see [17] published on the consumers' willingness to use mobile financial services have used either the original (i.e., perceived usefulness and perceived ease of use; [10]) or modified versions of the TAM (i.e., perceived risk, perceived compatibility, perceived cost and other drivers) as a primary theoretical lens. Although the former has good explanatory and predictive power (that is, it could explain 40% of behavioral intention for accepting a new technology; [23]), the latter enables us to meet the specifics of mobile payment characteristics [24].

Therefore, we follow on Lin et al. [11] who introduced the TRAM – an integrated model that further advances the logic of TAM by simultaneously examining various explanatory determinants of how users come to accept and use mobile payments. Instead of reporting about direct effects of different adoption drivers, similar to Gupta and Dhingra [14] we argue that distinctive (i.e., independent, mediating and moderating) roles should be recognized to demistify the causal nature of adoption drivers.

2.3 Perceived Mobility and the Usage of Mobile Payments

Perceived mobility is an important system-based antecedent in the study of mobile learning [25] and mobile commerce [26] that includes convenience, expediency and immediacy [27]. As the most significant characteristic of mobile payments [28], perceived mobility represents an enabler of access to mobile financial services, and therefore could be understood as a prerequisite or precondition for the consumers' intention to use mobile payments.

Interestingly, previous studies have rarely included perceived mobility into the TAM of explaining the consumers' mobile payment adoption behavior [24]. However, with an exception of Kim et al. [8], existing evidence showed that perceived mobility has a positive effect on perceived ease of use [29]. Likewise, it is positively related to perceived usefulness of mobile financial services [30]. As these constructs constitute the original TAM that measures the intention to use information technology services, we assume accordingly that perceived mobility might have a direct influence on the respective mobile payment adoption behavior. Therefore, we hypothesize the following:

H1: Perceived mobility is positively related with the intention to use mobile payments.

In addition to assuming that perceived mobility (or other commonly studied drivers of adoption) exemplifies a direct effect on the outcome variable of our interest [22], scholars have recently shown an increasing interest for revealing the underlying mechanisms (such as perceived usefulness and perceived ease of use [29]) that potentially drive consumers' mobile payment adoption behavior. Specifically, we suggest that mobile payment knowledge (i.e., a combination of the experience, training, and knowledge the individual has regarding mobile payment technology; [9]) plays an intervening role in the relationship between perceived mobility and intention to use mobile payments.

In line with TRAM [11], we introduce perceived mobility as an initiative (technology-related) predictor that potentially influence the (consumer-centric) perceived experience of using mobile technology, which further determines the behavioral intention to adopt and use mobile payments [13]. Individuals, who feel technologically ready, are prone to get more familiar and acquainted to mobile payment services, and thus eventually increase their intention to use mobile payments. Their counterparts, that is, non-tech savvy individuals who feel less enthusiastic about mobile payments, are expected to continue with ignoring the usage of mobile payment services in the future. In other words, we argue that individuals' technology-related beliefs can affect whether and how they experience and use mobile technologies [31]. Knowledgeable users should not be troubled when using the mobile payment channel [8]. The presence of mobile experience will reduce their anxiety and increase the enjoyment of mobile payments, thereby increasing their intention to use it [9]. Thus, we propose the following:

H2: Mobile payment knowledge mediates the relationship between perceived mobility and the intention to use mobile payments.

2.4 Positive and Negative Determinants of the Relationship Between Perceived Mobility and the Usage of Mobile Payments

Additional insights about constructs of our interest and their contingency (i.e., interactive) relationships are possible by introducing moderator variables. Up to date, only a few studies examined boundary conditions of the intention to adopt mobile payments (for a review see [17]). Although we could theorize about a large number of possible moderators (that is, positive and negative determinants of the focal relationship), we decided to focus on the most frequently examined T(R)AM variables in order to remain parsimonious. However, we understand and approach these variables as contingent (and not as predictor) variables.

Previous research has been primarily focused on positive determinants of the intention to use mobile payments [24]. *Perceived usefulness* (i.e., "the degree to which a person believes that using a particular system will enhance his or her job performance"; [10]) has been widely studied as a central variable in the TAM. It describes how consumers believe that mobile payment technology is useful and beneficial to them [8] and can promote their task performance [9]. Perceived usefulness has been reported to have a direct effect on adoption intention [24]. However, when examining the indirect effect of the perceived mobility on the intention to use mobile payments via mobile payment knowledge, we find it meaningful to examine the contextual nature of perceived usefulness. Specifically, if consumers find mobile payment applications useful in managing their financial transactions, the impact of mobile payment knowledge on the intention to use will be additionally strengthened. However, if they do not recognize the perceived usefulness of the mobile apps, this could lead to a substantially lower intention to use mobile payment services.

Similar occurrence is assumed for the *perceived compatibility* (i.e., the easiness of adopting mobile payments from the user's perspective; [22]), another positive determinant of the intention to adopt mobile payments for managing personal finance. It refers to how mobile payments are in line with everyday life habits of the consumer [22]. Existing evidence indicates that perceived compatibility is a strong driver of the mobile payment adoption [32, 33]. If consumers perceive a mobile payment service as such that it does not require them to undertake extensive lifestyle changes [22], then we could expect that a more positive relationship occurs between mobile payment knowledge and intention to use mobile payments. On the other hand, if mobile payments are not consistent with values and current needs of potential consumers [34], the focal relationship will be weakened. Accordingly, we hypothesize the following:

H3: Positive determinants (i.e., [a] the perceived compatibility and [b] the perceived usefulness of mobile payments) are second-stage moderators of the relationship between perceived mobility and the intention to use mobile payments via mobile payment knowledge.

Negative determinants of the relationship between perceived mobility and the usage of mobile payments have been less studied in the respective literature. *Perceived risk* (i.e., perceived exposure to privacy, financial and performance losses; [21]) causes feelings related to uncertainty and negative consequences [16] thus negatively affecting the behavioral intention to use mobile payments [35]. Specifically, when consumers experience higher possibility of unfavorable outcomes while using mobile payment services (e.g. lack of confidentiality between user and service provider for privacy, unauthorized access of data, the possibility of performing wrong transactions, and authenticity of service providers; [14]), their mobile payment knowledge would not contribute to the adoption intention as in the situation where perceived risk is rather low. In other words, the presence or absence of perceived risk causes different behavioral intentions towards mobile payment services [36].

Perceived cost (i.e., "the extent to which a person believes that using mobile payments will cost money"; [37]) is another important negative determinant or barrier that potentially reduces the willingness to adopt mobile payment services [22, 28]. Consumers who expect that the usage of mobile payments will lead to their financial loss (e.g., a handset [hardware/software] cost, subscription cost, service cost, and communication cost), would be less prone to put their mobile payment knowledge into action, that is, would hesitate to use the mobile payments. However, their counterparts, who are not perceiving such costs as problematic, are expected to increase the level of mobile payment usage. This leads us to the final hypothesis:

H4: Negative determinants (i.e., [a] the perceived risk and [b] the perceived cost of mobile payments) are second-stage moderators of the relationship between perceived mobility and the intention to use mobile payments via mobile payment knowledge.

Figure 1 shows the estimated model with hypothesized relationships for our study.

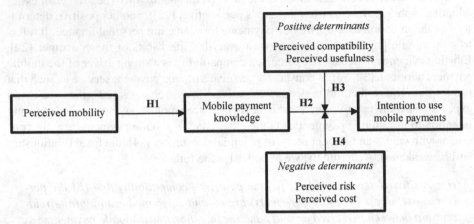

Fig. 1. The research model

3 Method

3.1 Sample

A cross-sectional field survey has been conducted at University of Zagreb, Croatia. Business students fully enrolled in the undergraduate program were invited to participate in the research. A questionnaire was created using Google Forms and the link had been accessible online (via social media platforms) for two weeks. The data collection process followed convenience sampling and resulted in 218 complete responses. The sample is gender biased (73.39% were females) and the majority of survey participants were 20 to 25 years old (91.28% of respondents). Their revenues were mainly below 400,00 EUR per month (71.10% of the sample), although a fifth of respondents reported to have a monthly budget of 650,00 EUR.

3.2 Measures

We introduced TAM [10] and TRAM [11] for studying individuals' preferences and acceptance of mobile-supported technology for managing mobile payments. However, following best practices the original theoretical frameworks have been revised to fit better with mobile payment challenges. We utilized a multiple-item method by adopting previously validated scales (i.e., a 5-point Likert type agreement statements; from *1 – completely disagree* to *5 – completely agree*) for the constructs of interest. In total, the questionnaire included 22 statements (covering seven constructs) supplemented with three socio-demographic questions. Multi-item scales applied were reliable as indicated by Cronbach's alphas reported to be above or close to the .70 threshold [38].

Perceived Mobility. We assessed perceived mobility as our independent variable using three items combinedly adopted from Kim et al. [8] and Liu et al. [24]. A sample item is "I believe that mobile payment is location independent" ($\alpha = .755$).

Mobile Payment Knowledge. This potential mediating variable was examined by adopting four-item scale validated by Kim et al. [8]. A sample item is "I would be confident to use m-banking for financial transactions" ($\alpha = .769$).

Perceived Compatibility. The first of two theory-derived positive determinants (i.e., boundary conditions or moderators) of the intention to use mobile payments has been assessed by using the original three item scale developed by Wu and Wang [39]. A sample item is "Using mobile payments is compatible with most aspects of my online transactions" ($\alpha = .820$).

Perceived Usefulness. The second positive determinant of the intention to use mobile payments recognized in the literature was measured by combining items from Koenig-Lewis et al. [32] and Liu et al. [24]. The sample item is "I think mobile payments are useful" ($\alpha = .688$).

Perceived Risk. In addition to positive, we also examined negative determinants of the intention to use mobile payments. Specifically, perceived risk has been examined as a moderator by adopting three-item scale from Liu et al. [24]. The sample item is "I am worried to use mobile payments because other people may be able to access my account" ($\alpha = .855$).

Perceived Cost. A scale for another theoretically important negative determinant of the intention to use mobile payments, that is, perceived cost, was taken from Wu and Wang [39]. Their three-item scale with a sample item "I think the equipment to use mobile payment service is expensive" showed the acceptable level of validity ($\alpha = .825$).

Intention to Use Mobile Payments. Our dependent variable measures behavioral intentions of respondents to use mobile payments in the near future. We adopted scale with three items [24]. The example item is "I would use mobile payments for my banking needs" ($\alpha = .883$).

Control Variables. We examined several demographic variables. For *gender*, we coded "male" as 1 and "female" as 2. We also measured a respondent's chronological *age* in years using four different age groups (under 20, from 20 to 25, from 25 to 30, and 30 +). In addition, respondents were asked to report about their mobile payment habits. Specifically, we were interested in their mobile payment experience and to find out (1) how frequently they use mobile payments, (2) for how long they already use mobile payments, as well as (3) what was their primary reason to start using mobile financial services. Aforementioned controls are chosen following best-practice recommendations for control variable usage [40].

3.3 Procedure

To further validate our research instrument and latent variables of interest (e.g. perceived mobility, mobile payment knowledge, intention to use mobile payments, and others), we conducted confirmatory factor analyses (CFAs), following the maximum-likelihood-estimation method in JASP 0.16.2. The CFA results indicated that 7-factor model ($\chi 2/df$

$= 328.708/188$; RMSEA $= .059$; CFI $= .941$) outperformed a single-factor model ($\chi 2/df$ $= 1346.322/209$; RMSEA $= .158$; CFI $= .523$). We took a conventional approach [41] that suggests retaining the items with a factor loading of .40 or greater. However, as only a single item measuring perceived usefulness of mobile payments did not meet the cut-off value ($\lambda = .370$), we decided to retain all of the original items. Such a decision is supported because (1) recommendation that factor loading greater than .30 is considered significant [42]; (2) the Cronbach alpha for the construct was nevertheless acceptable ($\alpha = .688$) and (3) the revised 7-factor model ($\chi 2/df = 293.416/168$; RMSEA $= .059$; CFI $= .943$) did not yield significant improvements in parameter estimates.

To address potential issues related to effects of common method bias [43] we ran Harman's single factor test, which revealed that no single factor explains the majority of the variance (i.e., 32.73% of the total variance was explained). Furthermore, we ran the Kolmogorov-Smirnov and Shapiro-Wilk normality tests. Results indicated the non-normality of our data. As the normality assumption is not essential for the validity of the bootstrap [44], we decided to test our research model and hypotheses using the PRO-CESS macro version 3.5 for SPSS [45]. We conducted hypotheses testing by examining: (a) a basic mediation relationship (i.e., the intervening role of consumer familiarity and experience; Model 4 in PROCESS templates), (b) the moderating role of positive determinants (i.e., perceived compatibility and perceived usefulness; Model 16 in PROCESS templates) and (c) the moderating role of negative determinants (i.e., perceived risk and perceived cost; Model 16 in PROCESS templates).

4 Results

4.1 Exploratory Data Analysis

Table 1 presents means, standard deviations, and correlations. Descriptive results indicate that an average student of business and economics has a high level of perceived mobility ($M = 4.393$, $SD = .674$) and even higher intention to use mobile payments ($M = 4.546$, $SD = .641$). Among examined determinants of the intention to use mobile payments as a delivery channel, the positive ones ($M = 4.488$, $SD = .630$ for perceived compatibility; $M = 4.642$, $SD = .499$ for perceived usefulness) are largely emphasized over negative moderators ($M = 3.217$, $SD = .960$ for perceived risk, $M = 2.109$, $SD = .866$ for perceived cost). In terms of the mobile payment knowledge, our respondents seem to be knowledgeable ($M = 4.006$, $SD = .843$).

Bivariate intercorrelations (Pearson's r) showed that independent variable (i.e., perceived mobility) is positively related to mediator variable (i.e., mobile payment knowledge; $r = .292$, $p < .01$) as well as to the outcome variable (i.e., intention to use; $r = .382$, $p < .01$). Additionally, the mediator variable is strongly positively associated with the outcome variable of our research model ($r = .550$, $p < .01$). Furthermore, a correlation analysis confirms a positive role of perceived compatibility ($r = .560$, $p < .01$) and perceived usefulness ($r = .501$, $p < .01$), as well as indicates that perceived risk ($r = -.233$, $p < .01$) and perceived cost ($r = -.286$, $p < .01$) might represent negative determinants of the intention to use mobile payments. Interestingly, a positive association that exists between positive determinants ($r = .632$, $p < .01$) is almost three times stronger than respective association between negative determinants ($r = .234$, $p < .01$).

Such results are indicative yet inconclusive and require further conditional process testing. We assessed the risk of multicollinearity between correlated independent variables by checking variance inflation factors (VIFs) and found all respective indicators to be acceptable (VIFs < 2).

Our research model (i.e., a modified version of the TRAM) explained significant variance in consumers' intentions to use mobile payments ($R^2 = .44$). As R^2 values above .20 indicate high predictive power in the consumer behavior discipline [42], we may conclude that the present research model offers a useful framework to predict consumers' intentions to use mobile payments.

Table 1. Correlation matrix with descriptives

	M	SD	1	2	3	4	5	6	7	8	9	10	11	12
1 Age	2.073	.352	–											
2 Gender	1.734	.443	.037	–										
3 Frequency of use	1.904	.948	.077	.005	–									
4 Duration of use	3.628	1.290	.101	.012	.389**	–								
5 Primary reason to use	2.724	1.024	.044	.163*	−.056	.149*	–							
6 Perceived mobility	4.393	.674	.085	.203**	.098	.185**	−.005	(.755)						
7 Mobile payment knowledge	4.006	.843	−.040	.013	.371**	.199**	−.084	.292**	(.769)					
8 Perceived compatibility	4.488	.630	.073	.153*	.290**	.269**	−.067	.476**	.466**	(.820)				
9 Perceived usefulness	4.642	.499	.063	.082	.284**	.224**	−.055	.505**	.360**	.632**	(.688)			
10 Perceived risk	3.217	.960	−.093	.079	−.215**	−.095	.027	−.178**	−.312**	−.123†	−.195**	(.855)		
11 Perceived cost	2.109	.866	−.092	−.049	−.231**	−.187**	.089	−.131†	−.254**	−.228**	−.297**	.234**	(.825)	
12 Intention to use	4.546	.641	−.015	.086	.337**	.297**	.031	.382**	.550**	.560**	.501**	−.223**	−.286**	(.883)

4.2 Direct and Indirect (Mediated) Effects

To start with, we ran a basic linear regression model with control variables (Template 0 in PROCESS) to determine whether perceived mobility and intention to use mobile payments are related. The ordinary least squares regression (OLS) resulted with a significant and positive beta coefficient ($B = .319$, $SE = .059$, $p < .01$) for perceived mobility as a predictor, providing support for our first hypothesis, i.e., the existence of a positive relationship between the independent and the outcome variables.

Next, we tested a basic mediation model (Template 4 in PROCESS) which (1) confirmed that perceived mobility has a positive direct effect on the intention to use mobile payments ($B = .213$, $SE = .055$, $BootSE = .055$, $BootCI$ [.104, .323]) and (2) revealed that perceived mobility affects the outcome variable indirectly via mobile payment knowledge (indirect effect $= .106$, $BootSE = .032$, $BootCI$ [.050, .172]). The co-occurrence of both direct and indirect effects (i.e., partial mediation) is in line with our assumptions, leading us to accept the second hypothesis.

4.3 Moderated Mediation Effects

Two sets of second-stage moderators (positive and negative determinants) were further tested separately using Model 16 in PROCESS templates [12] to additionally explain what might influence the focal mediation relationship. The moderated mediation analysis of positive determinants revealed that the perceived compatibility is a significant moderator (interaction effect $= .161$, $BootSE = .082$, $p < .05$) and the perceived usefulness of mobile payments' usage an insignificant boundary condition (interaction effect $= .148$, $BootSE = .108$, n.s.). Simple slopes analysis (Fig. 2) revealed that the slopes of the relationship at the low, medium and high levels of perceived compatibility are significantly different from zero, confirming that the intension to use mobile payments will be the highest when individuals perceive a high compatibility of the mobile technology with their lifestyle. Therefore, we may conclude that our H3a is supported. However, no evidence was found to not reject the H3b.

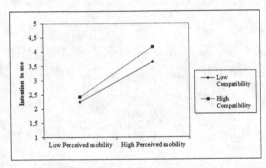

Fig. 2. Perceived mobility x Compatibility for the intention to use of mobile payments

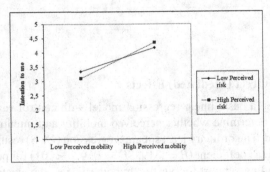

Fig. 3. Perceived mobility x Perceived Risk for the intention to use of mobile payments

Regarding the negative determinates, the same procedure was followed; we found perceived risk to be a significant moderator (interaction effect $= .131$, $BootSE = .040$, $p < .01$), while perceived cost of mobile payments' usage did not satisfy the significance threshold (interaction effect $= .032$, $BootSE = .051$, n.s.). Simple slopes analysis (Fig. 3) revealed that the slopes of the relationship at the low, medium and high levels of perceived risk are significantly different from zero, confirming that the intension to use mobile payments will be the lowest when individuals perceive high levels of risk. Accordingly, we were able to confirm the H4a, and had to reject our H4b.

Finally, tests of the full (a second-stage moderated mediation) models did not provide significant results. An exception was reported in the case of the conditional process model that included perceived risk as a moderator, for which a conditional indirect effect, that is, an index of partial moderated mediation, was positive and significant (index $= .044$, $BootSE = .023$, $BootCI$ [.001, .090]). In other words, we can additionally confirm that only the perceived risk is a boundary condition when mobile payment knowledge mediates the focal relationship between perceived mobility (i.e., an independent variable) and the intention to use mobile payments (i.e., an outcome variable).

5   Discussion

The present study examined an underlying mechanism (i.e., mobile payment knowledge) that drives the association between perceived mobility and intention to use mobile payments. We found empirical evidence for partial mediation, where direct and indirect effects coexist and simultaneously influence the outcome variable. In other words, both perceived mobility and mobile payment knowledge are positive drivers of the mobile payment adoption. Following the recommendation suggested by Rungtusanatham et al. [46], we additionally explored the significance of specific indirect effects above and beyond the total indirect effect. Conditional process analyses (i.e., moderation) confirmed that perceived compatibility and perceived risk represent significant positive and negative determinants, respectively. However, perceived usefulness and perceived cost of usage were non-significant antecedents. Moreover, only perceived risk was found to be a significant boundary condition when running moderated mediation models.

5.1   Theoretical Implications

A three-fold contribution is made to the understanding of mobile payment adoption. First, we clarified theoretical underpinnings of the antecedents (both enablers and inhibitors) of the intention to use mobile payments. Thus, we managed to move beyond predominant studies which addressed the direct effects on mobile payments adoption rather than dealing with moderating/mediating effects [22]. By using TRAM as a baseline for our comprehensive research model, we clearly delineated the role and causal nature of different constructs of interest and offered a deeper understanding of the mobile payment phenomenon that is currently lacking in the literature [13]. Specifically, our study followed a pioneering work that recently introduced TRAM into the FinTech literature [47], as well as extended the latest attempt of providing the hierarchy of adoption factors [13]. We shed a light on mobile payment knowledge – an important factor that has not been studied frequently. Our study not only confirmed insight that mobile users with a high level of mobile payment knowledge are likely to use the mobile payment systems more often [8], yet recognized it as an underlying mechanism driving the relationship between perceived mobility and intention to use mobile payments.

Second, our data on consumers' mobile payment behaviors and preferences were obtained from a cohort of digital natives (i.e., young consumers from generation Z;

[48]) and cover the EU member country (i.e., Croatia) that has not been previously investigated. Thus, we were able to validate our comprehensive research model and extend the regional scope of the related research, going beyond the mainstream findings focused on generation Y consumers [49]) and emerging/developing markets such as China and India [6, 7].

Third, a regression-based conditional process analysis [12] has been applied as a novel methodological approach to the field. As such, we made a distinctive step from using structural equation modelling (SEM) as a preferred mode of statistical analysis to validate TAM [6]. Instead of going for the inclusiveness of SEM where the entire system of equations is calculated through iteration, PROCESS macro for SPSS enabled us to estimate the parameters of each equation separately [50]. Such an approach is aligned with our theorizing; we were interested and focused on gaining the insights about specific roles of positive and negative determinants (that is, interactions between specific sets of constructs) and not on the full model perse.

5.2   Practical Implications

The intention to use mobile payments is of a sizable interest to practitioners [51]; they can benefit substantially from enhanced understanding of the underlying mechanism(s), as well as enablers and inhibitors of the mobile payment adoption. Our study showed that young consumers – digital natives who are knowledgeable about mobile payments – are more likely to adopt and use mobile payments in their everyday transactions.

Therefore, proponents of the mobile payment services (e.g. policymakers and mobile financial services' providers) should be interested to invest in digital/mobile and financial literacy of potential consumers. By educating potential consumers, they can stimulate and increase mobile financial inclusion. In addition, mobile payment services require novel business models and should be additionally modernized to meet the lifestyle characteristics and requirements of the generation Z consumers. Last but not the least, potential risks of mobile payment usage should be explained and minimized, to decrease the financial vulnerability that is often related with younger consumers [52].

5.3   Study Limitations and Future Research

The findings should be evaluated taking into account research limitations. To start with, the regression analyses have been conducted on a student sample of digital natives. Without losing generation Z consumers from our sight, it would be interesting to study non-students from the same generational cohort to see whether and to what extent university education has an impact on the readiness and willingness to adopt mobile payments. Moreover, it would be interesting to further validate and generalize our findings by using and comparing different cohorts of mobile payment users across countries.

Another limitation is related to the measurement aspect of research design. Although the majority of studies hypothesizing about mediating relationships utilized cross-sectional data [53], the longitudinal dataset is more appropriate for testing causal relationships. On a related note, despite of showing that the common method bias is not present within our single-source dataset, future research should intend to collect data from different sources (e.g. objective information retrieved from mobile payment systems).

Finally, we decided to use a less optimal threshold value of .30 for assessing the calculated factor loadings. Only one of our items had a 'questionable' communality score of .37. Nevertheless, it still remained in line with Hair et al. [42], who recommended to suppress factor loadings that are less than .30. As all other factor loadings were greater than .40 (and even above .60), we considered our measurement instruments to be stable [54].

Acknowledgements. This publication is based upon work from COST Action 19130 Fintech and Artificial Intelligence in Finance, supported by COST (European Cooperation in Science and Technology), www.cost.eu.

References

1. Hu, Z., Ding, S., Li, S., Chen, L., Yang, S.: Adoption intention of fintech services for bank users: an empirical examination with an extended technology acceptance model. Symmetry **11**, 340 (2019). https://doi.org/10.3390/sym11030340
2. Federal Deposit Insurance Corporation (FDIC): How America banks: household use of banking and financial services. FDIC Survey (2019)
3. ReportLinker: Global digital banking market to reach $30.1 Billion by 2026. https://www.globenewswire.com/news-release/2022/03/04/2397089/0/en/Global-Digital-Banking-Market-to-Reach-30-1-Billion-by-2026.html (2022)
4. Himel, T.A., Ashraf, S., Bappy, T.A., Abir, T., Morshed, K., Hossain, M.: Users' attitude and intention to use mobile financial services in Bangladesh: an empirical study. South Asian J. Mark. **2**(1), 72–96 (2021). https://doi.org/10.1108/SAJM-02-2021-0015
5. Munoz-Leiva, F., Climent-Climent, S., Liebana-Cabanillas, F.: Determinants of intention to use the mobile banking apps: an extension of the classic TAM model. Spanish J. Mark. – ECIS, **21**(1), 25–38 (2017). https://doi.org/10.1016/j.sjme.2016.12.001
6. Abdullah, M., Khan, M.N.: Determining mobile payment adoption: A systematic literature search and bibliometric analysis. Cogent Bus. Manag. **8**, 1893245 (2021). https://doi.org/10.1080/23311975.2021.1893245
7. Shaikh, A.A., Alamoudi, H., Alharthi, M., Glavee-Geo, R.: Advances in mobile financial services: a review of the literature and future research directions. Int. J. Bank Mark. **41**(1), 1–33 (2023). https://doi.org/10.1108/IJBM-06-2021-0230
8. Kim, C., Mirusmonov, M., Lee, I.: An empirical examination of factors influencing the intention to use mobile payment. Comput. Hum. Behav. **26**(3), 310–322 (2010). https://doi.org/10.1016/j.chb.2009.10.013
9. Al-Qudah, A.A., Al-Okaily, M., Alqudah, G., Ghazlat, A.: Mobile payment adoption in the time of the COVID-19 pandemic. Electron. Commer. Res. (2022)https://doi.org/10.1007/s10660-022-09577-1
10. Davis, F.D.: Perceived usefulness, perceived ease of use, and user acceptance of information technology. MIS Q. **13**(3), 319–339 (1989). https://doi.org/10.2307/249008
11. Lin, C.-H., Shih, H.-Y., Sher, P.J.: Integrating technology readiness into technology acceptance: the TRAM model. Psychol. Mark. **24**(7), 641–657 (2007). https://doi.org/10.1002/mar.20177
12. Hayes, A.F.: Introduction to Mediation, Moderation, and Conditional Process Analysis: A Regression-Based Approach. Guilford Press, New York (2022)
13. Sinha, N., Singh, N.: Moderating and mediating effect of perceived experience on merchant's behavioral intention to use mobile payments services. J. Fin. Serv. Mark. (2022)https://doi.org/10.1057/s41264-022-00163-y

14. Gupta, S., Dhingra, S.: Modeling the key factors influencing the adoption of mobile financial services: an interpretive structural modeling approach. J. Financ. Serv. Mark. **27**, 96–110 (2022). https://doi.org/10.1057/s41264-021-00101-4

15. Lee, I., Shin, Y.J.: Fintech: ecosystem, business models, investment decisions, and challenges. Bus. Horiz. **61**(1), 35–46 (2018). https://doi.org/10.1016/j.bushor.2017.09.003

16. Hasan, R., Ashfaq, M., Shao L.: Evaluating drivers of fintech adoption in the Netherlands. Glob. Bus. Rev. (2021)https://doi.org/10.1177/09721509211027402

17. Ernst & Young: Global Fintech Adoption Index 2019. Ernst & Young, London (2019)

18. Gupta, S., Yun, H., Xu, H., Kim, H.W.: An exploratory study on mobile banking adoption in Indian metropolitan and urban areas: a scenario-based experiment. Inf. Technol. Dev. **23**(1), 127–152 (2017). https://doi.org/10.1080/02681102.2016.1233855

19. Guermond, G.: Whose money? Digital remittances, mobile money and fintech in Ghana. J. Cult. Econ. **15**(4), 436–451 (2022). https://doi.org/10.1080/17530350.2021.2018347

20. de Albuquerque, J.P., Diniz, E.H., Cernev, A.K.: Mobile payments: a scoping study of the literature and issues for future research. Inf. Dev. **32**(3), 527–553 (2014). https://doi.org/10.1177/0266666914557338

21. Nguyen, Y.T.H., Tapanainen, T., Nguyen, H.T.T.: Reputation and its consequences in Fintech services: the case of mobile banking. Int. J. Bank Mark. (2022)https://doi.org/10.1108/IJBM-08-2021-0371

22. Ha, K.-H., Canedoli, A., Baur, A.W., Bick, M.: Mobile banking — insights on its increasing relevance and most common drivers of adoption. Electron. Mark. **22**, 217–227 (2012). https://doi.org/10.1007/s12525-012-0107-1

23. Legris, P., Ingham, J., Collerette, P.: Why do people use information technology? A critical review of the technology acceptance model. Inf. Manag. **40**(3), 191–204 (2003). https://doi.org/10.1016/S0378-7206(01)00143-4

24. Liu, Y., Wang, M., Huang, D., Huang, Q., Yang, H., Li, Z.: The impact of mobility, risk, and cost on the users' intention to adopt mobile payments. IseB **17**(2–4), 319–342 (2019). https://doi.org/10.1007/s10257-019-00449-0

25. Huang, J.-H., Lin, Y.-R., Chuang, S.-T.: Elucidating user behavior of mobile learning: a perspective of the extended technology acceptance model. Electron. Libr. **25**(5), 585–598 (2007). https://doi.org/10.1108/02640470710829569

26. Anckar, B., D'Incau, D.: Value creation in mobile commerce: findings from a consumer survey. J. Inf. Technol. Theory Appl. **4**(1), 43–64 (2002)

27. Seppälä, P., Alamäki, H.: Mobile learning in teacher training. J. Comput. Assist. Learn. **19**(3), 330–335 (2003). https://doi.org/10.1046/j.0266-4909.2003.00034.x

28. Dahlberg, T., Mallat, N., Ondrus, J., Zmijewska, A.: Past, present and future of mobile payments research: a literature review. Electron. Commer. Res. Appl. **7**(2), 165–181 (2008). https://doi.org/10.1016/j.elerap.2007.02.001

29. Yen, Y.-S., Wu, F.-S.: Predicting the adoption of mobile financial services: the impacts of perceived mobility and personal habit. Comput. Hum. Behav. **65**, 31–42 (2016). https://doi.org/10.1016/j.chb.2016.08.017

30. Kwon, S.J., Park, E., Kim, K.J.: What drives successful social networking services: a comparative analysis of user acceptance of Facebook and Twitter. Soc. Sci. J. **51**(4), 534–544 (2014). https://doi.org/10.1016/j.soscij.2014.04.005

31. Blut, M., Wang, C.: Technology readiness: a meta-analysis of conceptualizations of the construct and its impact on technology usage. J. Acad. Mark. Sci. **48**(4), 649–669 (2019). https://doi.org/10.1007/s11747-019-00680-8

32. Koenig-Lewis, N., Palmer, A., Moll, A.: Predicting young consumers' take up of mobile banking services. Int. J. Bank Mark. **28**(5), 410–432 (2010). https://doi.org/10.1108/02652321011064917

33. Lin, H.F.: An empirical investigation of mobile banking adoption: the effect of innovation attributes and knowledge-based trust. Int. J. Inf. Manage. **3**(3), 252–260 (2010). https://doi. org/10.1016/j.ijinfomgt.2010.07.006
34. Püschel, J., Mazzon, J.A., Hernandez, J.M.C.: Mobile banking: proposition of an integrated adoption intention framework. Int. J. Bank Mark. **28**(5), 389–409 (2010). https://doi.org/10. 1108/02652321011064908
35. Wu, J., Lin, L., Huang, L.: Consumer acceptance of mobile payment across time. Ind. Manag. Data Syst. **117**(8), 1761–1776 (2017). https://doi.org/10.1108/IMDS-08-2016-0312
36. Unnikrishnan, R., Jagannathan, L.: Do perceived risk and trust affect consumer adoption of mobile payments? A study of Indian consumers. South Asian J. Manag. **25**(4), 74–100 (2018)
37. Luarn, P., Lin, H.H.: Toward an understanding of the behavioral intention to use mobile banking. Comput. Hum. Behav. **21**(6), 873–891 (2005). https://doi.org/10.1016/j.chb.2004. 03.003
38. Nunnally, J.C.: Psychometric Theory. McGraw-Hill, New York (1978)
39. Wu, J.-H., Wang, S.-C.: What drives mobile commerce? An empirical evaluation of the revised technology acceptance model. Inf. Manag. **42**(5), 719–729 (2005). https://doi.org/10.1016/j. im.2004.07.001
40. Bernerth, J.B., Aguinis, H.: A critical review and best-practice recommendations for control variable usage. Pers. Psychol. **69**(1), 229–283 (2016). https://doi.org/10.1111/peps.12103
41. Cabrera-Nguyen, P.: Author guidelines or reporting scale development and validation results in the journal of the society for social work and research. J. Soc. Soc. Work Res. **1**(2), 99–103 (2010). https://doi.org/10.5243/jsswr.2010.8
42. Hair, J.F., Jr., Anderson, R.E., Tatham, R.L., Black, W.C.: Multivariate Data Analysis. Prentice Hall, Upper Saddle River (1998)
43. Podsakoff, P.M., MacKenzie, S.B., Lee, J.-Y., Podsakoff, N.P.: Common method biases in behavioral research: a critical review of the literature and recommended remedies. J. Appl. Psychol. **88**(5), 879–903 (2003). https://doi.org/10.1037/0021-9010.88.5.879
44. Yuan, Y., MacKinnon, D.P.: Robust mediation analysis based on median regression. Psychol. Methods **19**(1), 1–20 (2014). https://doi.org/10.1037/a0033820
45. Hayes, A.F.: The PROCESS macro for SPSS, SAS, and R. https://www.processmacro.org/ index.html (2022a)
46. Rungtusanatham, M., Miller, J.W., Boyer, K.K.: Theorizing, testing, and concluding for mediation in SCM research: tutorial and procedural recommendations. J. Oper. Manag. **32**(3), 99–113 (2014). https://doi.org/10.1016/j.jom.2014.01.002
47. Martens, M., Roll, O., Elliott, R.: Testing the technology readiness and acceptance model for mobile payments across Germany and South Africa. Int. J. Innov. Technol. Manag. **14**(6), 1750033 (2017). https://doi.org/10.1142/S021987701750033X
48. Agardi, I., Alt, M.A.: Do digital natives use mobile payment differently than digital immigrants? A comparative study between generation X and Z. Electron. Comm. Res. (2022)https:// doi.org/10.1007/s10660-022-09537-9
49. Tan, E., Lau, J.L.: Behavioural intention to adopt mobile banking among the millennial generation. Young Consumers **17**(1), 18–31 (2016). https://doi.org/10.1108/YC-07-2015-00537
50. Hayes, A.F., Montoya, A.K., Rockwood, N.J.: The analysis of mechanisms and their contingencies: PROCESS versus structural equation modeling. Australas. Mark. J. **25**(1), 76–81 (2017). https://doi.org/10.1016/j.ausmj.2017.02.001
51. McKinsey: The 2020 McKinsey Global Payments Report, https://www.mckinsey.com (2020)
52. Seldal, M.M.N., Nyhus, E.K.: Financial vulnerability, financial literacy, and the use of digital payment technologies. J. Consum. Policy **45**, 281–306 (2022). https://doi.org/10.1007/s10 603-022-09512-9

53. Maxwell, S.E., Cole, D.A.: Bias in cross-sectional analyses of longitudinal mediation. Psychol. Methods **12**, 23–44 (2007). https://doi.org/10.1037/1082-989X.12.1.23
54. Guadagnoli, E., Velicer, W.F.: Relation of sample size to the stability of component patterns. Psychol. Bull. **103**(2), 265–275 (1988). https://doi.org/10.1037/0033-2909.103.2.265

Author Index

A
Abhishta, Abhishta 97

C
Clapham, Benjamin 17

D
Dzelalija, Petar 117

G
Gomber, Peter 36

H
Hussain, Walayat 82

I
Ivanisevic Hernaus, Ana 117

J
Joosten, Reinoud 97

K
Koch, Jascha-Alexander 36
Koefer, Franziska 52

L
Lausen, Jens 17
Lemken, Ivo 52

M
Manchanda, Chinmay 82
Mathuva, David 68
Meijer, Koen 97

N
Ng, Siu Lung 1
Ngaruiya, Jane 68

O
Obi, Pat 68

P
Pauls, Jan 52

R
Rabhi, Fethi 1, 82
Rabhi, Latif 82

Printed in the United States
by Baker & Taylor Publisher Services

Printed in the United States
by Baker & Taylor Publisher Services